Teamwork in Foreign Languages

Selected Papers from the 2001 Central States Conference

Edited by
Larbi Oukada
Indiana University-Purdue University
Indianapolis, IN
and
Alan Garfinkel
Purdue University
West Lafayette, IN

Authors
Jessie Carduner, Rebecca L. Chism, and Ann Masters Salomone
Helena Curtain and Carol Ann Pesola Dahlberg
Marie Trayer
Linda Quinn Allen
Kristin Hoyt-Oukada
Donna Reseigh Long and Janice L. Macián
Sydney Norton
Lisa M. Calvin
John I. Liontas
Karen Hardy Cárdenas

Publisher: Lee Bradley
             Assistant Professor of French, Emeritus
             Valdosta State University
             Valdosta, GA 31698

Printer: Colson Printing Company
             711 North Oak Street
             Valdosta, GA 31601

ISBN: 1-883640-10-5

© Central States Conference on theTeaching of Foreign Languages
  Diane Ging, Executive Director
  Post Office Box 21531
  Columbus, OH 43221-0531
  Telephone 614-529-0109; facsmile 614-529-0321
  dging@iwaynet.net; http://centralstates.cc

7 2 3 L B 0 9 8 7 6 5 4 3 2 1

Contents

Preface vi

Introduction: Teamwork Wins the Race viii
Alan Garfinkel and Larbi Oukada

Programmatic Planning

1 **Teamwork in Teacher Training: Key to
   Collaboration at Kent** 1
   Jessie Carduner, Rebecca L. Chism, & Ann
   Masters Salomone

2 **Dangerous Assumptions in Early Language
   Learning Programs** 17
   Helena Curtain & Carol Ann Pesola Dahlberg

3 **IN-VISION: An Innovative Model for K-12
   Spanish in Rural Schools** 27
   Marie Trayer

Curricular Issues

4 **Standards-Based Foreign Language Learning
   and Teachers' Pedagogical Beliefs** 33
   Linda Quinn Allen

5 **Development and Dissemination of the Indiana
   Academic Standards for Foreign Languages:
   Teacher Teamwork at the Forefront of the Project** 47
   Kristin Hoyt-Oukada

Instructional Approaches

6 **Writing Activities and Assessments for Today's Classroom: A Step-by-Step Approach** 57
Donna Reseigh Long & Janice L. Macián

7 **Teamwork in Exploring the Target Culture: Creating a Foreign Language Newspaper** 69
Sydney Norton

8 **Language Learning and Cultural Adjustment: Information and Implications for ESL/Foreign Language Instructors** 75
Lisa M. Calvin

9 **Playing with a Purpose: Defining the Issues** 87
John I. Liontas

10 **Oh, What a Tangled Web ... Teaching Foreign Languages Online** 103
Karen Hardy Cárdenas

Review and Acceptance Procedures
Central States Conference 2001 Report

The *Central State Conference Report* is a refereed volume of selected papers from the annual Central States Conference on the Teaching of Foreign Languages. Abstracts for sessions are first submitted to the Program Chair. The Program Chair, in conjunction with the annual program committee, reads, evaluates, and then selects the sessions that will be presented at the annual conference.

Once the sessions have been selected, presenters are contacted by the editors of the *CSC Report* and invited to submit a manuscript for possible publication in that volume. Copies of the publication guidelines are sent to presenters who express interest in submitting a manuscript based on their presentation. Once all references to the authors and their affiliations have been removed, manuscripts are read and evaluated by members of the Editorial Board. These individuals are experts in second language acquisition or foreign language methodology. Reviewers are asked to recommend that a manuscript (1) be published in its current form, (2) be published after particular revisions have been made, or (3) not be published. The Editors make all final publishing decisions. The names and affiliations of the Editors and members of the Editorial Board are listed below.

Editors

Larbi Oukada	Indiana University-Purdue University Indianapolis, IN
Alan Garfinkel	Purdue University West Lafayette, IN

Editorial Board

Lee Bradley	Valdosta State University, Valdosta, GA
Page Curry	Bellarmine College, Louisville, KY
Rick Weber	Transylvania University, Lexington, KY
Stacia Pleasants	Purdue University, West Lafayette, IN
Paul C. Miller	Purdue University, West Lafayette, IN
Marcela Rodríguez de van Olphen	Purdue University, West Lafayette, IN

Preface

After a ten-year absence, the *Central State Conference on the Teaching of Foreign Languages (CSC)* returns to Indianapolis, Indiana, for its 33rd annual meeting. This year's theme, "Teamwork Wins the Race," encourages us to think about the effects teamwork has on achieving goals. The Indianapolis Colts, the Indiana Pacers, the winning teams at the Indy 500, Brickyard 400, and the United States Grand Prix all rely on teamwork to produce a winning environment. Business and educational institutions depend on teamwork to produce outstanding products.

Sidney Taurel, CEO of the Eli Lilly Pharmaceutical Company, emphasizes in his keynote speech the need in world trade for cross-cultural teamwork in order to achieve goals. Dena Bachman, Coordinator of Foreign Languages for the St. Joseph, Missouri schools, speaks of teamwork as being necessary to create the BIG picture. This year's *CSC* annual meeting remains faithful to the teamwork concept. Some 17 double-play sessions allow participants to see two sessions in the same time block as presenters are sharing their time slots.

Some 21 workshops, 200 sessions, and special workshops by ACTFL and the AATSP provide a variety of topics featuring standards, articulation, methods and techniques, and culture. Focus sessions highlight the New Visions of ACTFL, and the Extension Workshop deals with the standards and lesson planning.

We can use teamwork as a point of unity. It is time that all language teachers work together in order to promote all languages. There is a need to address world languages and cultures through a team effort. Teamwork in our profession serves to promote foreign language study. Working with fellow language teachers, we can make an effort to collaborate and do creative, team based teaching. Students will be the benefactors of our team effort, and students will imitate our efforts to be team players. If we work as a team, everyone wins. Teamwork does indeed win the race!

Tom Alsop
2001 Program Chair

CSC 2000–2002 Officers and Directors

Chair, Board of Directors	Richard Kalfus, MO
Vice Chair, Board of Directors	Patrick T. Raven, WI
Executive Director	Diane Ging, OH
Recording Secretary	Lynne Overesch-Maister, KS
Program Chair	Tom Alsop, IN
Assistant Program Chair	Rosalie Vermette, IN
Local Chair	Cheryl Rich, IN
Editor, Central Connection	Millie Mellgren, MI
JNCL/NCLIS Delegate	Jody Thrush, WI
ACTFL Executive Council Delegate	Paul Sandrock, WI
Director	John J. Janc, MN
Director	Martie Semmer, CO
Director	Richard Weber, KY
Director	Sharon Rapp, AR
Director	Pam Seccombe, WI
Director	Phyllis Van Buren, MN
Director	Marie Trayer, NE
Director	Donna Clementi, WI
Director	Anne Nerenz, MI

Introduction

Teamwork in Foreign Languages Wins the Race

Our readers see the conference theme listed as the title of this introduction and are fully entitled to ask, "What race?" Is all of this a mere ploy to create a public relations effect by linking the conference and its *Report* to the venue's well-known passion for automobile racing? Your editors respectfully deny the charge. We further note that both, the conference and its *Report* are demonstrations of the truth to be found in the conference theme. Let us explain.

One cannot become a "member" of the *Central States Conference on the Teaching of Foreign Languages (CSC).* Individuals link themselves with *CSC* through attendance at events it sponsors. *CSC* is not an association, not a club, and not an honorary society. It is a non-profit corporation organized for the purpose of providing professional development for foreign language teachers in seventeen states from Ohio to Colorado and from our northern borders to Arkansas. As such, it began thirty-three years ago by sponsoring a single meeting for all the foreign language teachers of the region each year. Since then, it has expanded to include the extension workshops, this *Report,* two annual award programs, and several other services to practicing classroom teachers of foreign languages at all levels. Because of its nature and its principal service of sponsoring the annual conference, *CSC* finds itself in a kind of a race every year. That is the race to attract enough teachers to make *CSC* fiscally viable. True, ours is a market economy, and *CSC* may indeed deserve its fate if it fails to attract a "market."

For just that reason, each year represents a race to the goal for *CSC.* The goal is to present an annual meeting that is professionally attractive enough to bring teachers from all seventeen central states and, thus, survive to plan for yet another year. Not surprisingly, achieving that goal (and winning that race) is not something done by one or two people alone. Each year the task, an ever-growing one, is subdivided and passed on to a large team of people. That team is usually formed by members of the host state language teachers' association in combination with the small but dedicated part-time paid staff of the *CSC,* just as it has been this year. The team set an ambitious attendance goal ("2001 for 2001") which, if fully achieved, would mean not only financial success for this year but the ability to make ample plans for succeeding years. This year, the team includes the two members of the *CSC* staff and a large number of Indiana Foreign Language Teachers Association members to handle the program, exhibits, local arrangements, and the *CSC Report.*

Teamwork is vital to the production of the *CSC Report* as well. This year's team efforts began with authors who, because of conference scheduling, worked under pressure to create a written version of their accepted presentations. They have produced a wide array of articles for *CSC* conferees, ranging from discussions on models for structuring foreign language education, to topics on the implementation of standards and related curricular implications, to particular strategies and techniques for developing language skills, to the purpose and use of games and technology in second language instruction.

Next, reviewers selected by the editors for their knowledge of the language education field and their years of practical classroom language teaching experience were asked to indicate strengths and weaknesses of each submission to facilitate inclusion of the best and most representative articles available. Finally, the editors worked to shape the accepted submissions into a synergy, hoping that it truly does represent more than the sum of its elements. We, the present editors, mean for this volume to provide both a portrait of the 2001 *CSC* annual meeting and a document that will be of some lasting value to the language teaching profession as a whole.

And so it is, for *CSC* in general, and for the *CSC Report* in particular, no one person can claim credit. Both are products of teams, and it is indeed true, here and elsewhere, that TEAMWORK IN FOREIGN LANGUAGES WINS THE RACE.

Larbi Oukada
Indiana University-Purdue University
Indianapolis, IN

Alan Garfinkel
Purdue University
West Lafayette, IN

1
Teamwork in Teacher Training: Key to Collaboration at Kent

Jessie Carduner
Rebecca L. Chism
Anne Masters Salomone
Kent State University

Communication is generally accepted as the ultimate goal of foreign language (FL) and second language (SL) study. Language texts (e.g., Manley, Smith, McMinn & Prévost, 1998) and methodology texts (e.g., Lee & VanPatten, 1995) and our national standards clearly reflect this emphasis. While communication as a language teaching goal is universally endorsed, little attention has been given to the need for communication among preservice and inservice teachers. Because of the unique nature of our discipline, opportunities for communication and collaboration may be rare.

Preservice K-12 FL/SL teachers are often isolated during their training because the skills they must develop are noticeably different from those of their peers in other content areas; inservice K-12 teachers may find themselves isolated due to the geographical location of their schools; and FL graduate teaching assistants (GTAs) may be isolated because they normally assume full responsibility for their foreign language classes, unlike GTAs in many other disciplines. To lessen this isolation in our Department of Modern and Classical Language Studies (MCLS) at Kent State University (KSU), we encourage communication among pre- and inservice FL/SL teachers–including GTAs–in the form of collaborative training and professional development, often supported by technology.

On Defining Collaboration

Given the theme of the 2001 Central States Conference, we thought it appropriate to collaborate on this paper. In fact, collaboration has become a much-espoused goal of teacher education, especially since the Holmes Group called for a change in "the working relationships, roles, and responsibilities within and between schools and universities so that their collaborative endeavors can assure the public of well-educated teachers for America's children" (1986, p. 87). FL researchers concur, stating that "Collaboration is the key to effective foreign language teacher education programs" (Wing, 1993, p. 182).

While we all agreed that collaboration is important, we soon realized that each of us interpreted the term differently. Others have also noticed the variety of ways in which the term *collaboration* has been interpreted (e.g., Dillenbourg, 1999; Friesen, 1997; and Olson, 1990). The problem of definition and interpretation likely stems from the fact that collaboration may occur at many different sites–in the schools, universities, and community– and may involve a varied range of collaborative partnerships, including teachers and students, consultants and teachers, or teachers and teachers (Christiansen, Goulet, Krentz & Maeers, 1997, p. xv).

In spite of these variations in venue and personnel, it is possible to identify certain characteristics common to all collaborative endeavors. Researchers seem to agree that collaborative situations (a) involve shared goals (e.g., Dillenbourg, 1999; Schwartz, 1990); (b) require symmetrical (perceived or actual) and trusting relationships among the participants (Kapuscinski, 1997; Nicholls, 1997); (c) should effect some sort of (positive) change (e.g., Christiansen et al., 1997; Nicholls, 1997); and (d) are synchronous and parallel in terms of the participants' contributions—unlike cooperation, which involves the division of labor (e.g., Dillenbourg, 1999; Nicholls, 1997).

Rationale for collaboration

For preservice K-12 teachers in Ohio, collaboration is clearly required by the Pathwise Assessment Criteria, Ohio's current classroom observation system for novice teachers. One of the four domains used to categorize teacher behavior and knowledge, Domain D3, states that teachers are to be evaluated on their ability to build "professional relationships with colleagues, to share teaching insights and to coordinate learning activities for students" (Educational Testing Service, 1995, p. 48). Justification exists for this mandate: Collaborative relationships among preservice teachers, their peers, their cooperating teachers, and their university supervisors have been shown to alleviate stress during field experiences, to increase effectiveness, and to encourage professional growth (Wadlington, Partridge, & Slaton, 1998).

New Ohio Department of Education licensure standards, effective July, 2002, will require that teachers earn a master's degree within 12 years of their initial licensure. This new mandate will ensure that preservice teachers' professional development does not cease once they become inservice teachers. The ruling is designed to promote more sharing of pedagogical practices and knowledge between schools and universities and the improvement of inservice teachers' language proficiency and cultural knowledge.

Unlike K-12 FL/SL teachers, GTAs receive very little or no training prior to teaching. Many or most of their teaching skills must be acquired on the job. Unfortunately, neither the GTAs nor the undergraduate students they teach can afford to wait for the GTA to acquire the necessary skills so vital to the department; their performance is vital to university language programs. Lee points out that the quality of their instruction affects the future academic and linguistic success of their students (1989, p. 6); and Nerenz, Herron, and Knop (1979) suggest that a student's decision to continue with foreign language study may very well depend on their first language course, often one taught by a GTA.

This experience needs to be positive for undergraduates and for the GTA. Boehrer and Sarkisian (1985) suggest that even for GTAs who do not intend to teach in the future, their self-esteem during graduate school is strongly influenced by their teaching performance. And, according to Worthen, GTAs who feel they do not have enough preparation or support use words such as "nervous wreck" and "frustrating" to describe their experiences (1992, p. 6).

To ensure that our GTAs feel supported and integrated into our department, we cultivate a collegial spirit that encourages GTA collaboration with peers and regular faculty during their time at Kent and beyond. At the same time, we try to plant the seeds for professional development for any who may later choose teaching as their profession.

Kent's Pedagogy Programs

Preservice K-12 Teachers

In 1998, the Ohio Department of Education approved our revised undergraduate teacher education curriculum, which closely follows the American Council on the Teaching of Foreign Languages (ACTFL) Guidelines for Foreign Language Teacher Education (ACTFL, 1988). All students now earn a B.A. degree in the College of Arts and Sciences (CAS), with majors in French, German, Latin, Russian, or Spanish and a minor in Education. The College of Education provides three inquiry seminars; all other courses are administered in CAS, including Computers for Second Language Teaching, Psychology of Language, Foreign Languages and Culture, two methods courses, student teaching and a fourth inquiry seminar.

Inservice K-12 Teachers

Kent's M.A. programs in French, German, Latin, and Spanish (Pedagogy Concentration) primarily serve inservice K-12 teachers by addressing their on-going needs. Classes are held once weekly after school hours, and coursework is classroom-relevant (e.g., Computers for Second Language Teaching; Teaching Literature and Culture).

Graduate Teaching Assistant Preparation

In the first semester of their M.A. programs, all GTAs, regardless of language and concentration area (literature, pedagogy, or translation) participate in a one-week, pre-term workshop, both in mixed and individual language sessions; attend a mixed language semester-long methods class for three hours of graduate credit; and attend weekly meetings with their language coordinator, who is also the instructor of the model class they observe for most of the semester.

Kent's Cultivation of Collaboration

Collaboration occurs for all pedagogy students and GTAs in each of the following categories, which often overlap and interrelate: teaching observations, micro-teaching, teacher reflection, supervision and coordination, and socialization into the profession.

Classroom observations of two types–observations of model teaching and peer observations–have long been an accepted practice of teacher training programs. According to Shaw, for example, "Lesson observation is . . . a vital part of the development and assessment of teaching skills" and "both trainee and mentor need to receive careful training . . . to ensure that observation is truly developmental" (1995, pp. 106-107). Preservice K-12 teachers spend 60 hours in schools observing veteran teachers for their methods classes and more time observing their cooperating teachers during their orientation to student teaching. They also observe their peers in classroom teaching situations, when lessons are videotaped for self- and peer-critique. This videotaping affords a closer examination of preservice teacher performance than observation alone. As noted by Struyk and McCoy (1993), videotape for evaluative purposes provides preservice teachers with specific information about their performance and can be viewed as many times as necessary. Videotape also provides a means for tracking overall growth and improvement in a less-threatening format (pp. 32-33) and provides preservice teachers with opportunities to analyze and critique performances, thereby strengthening essential skills necessary for professional awareness and growth (Struyk, Cole, & Kinder, 1995).

For inservice K-12 teachers, videos of master teachers serve as models in M.A. pedagogy classes and are used to record class presentations that students self- and peer-critique. Students are also encouraged to observe each other in their home schools. This type of peer observation may, in fact, prolong their professional lives. Research shows that new teachers involved in a mentoring program that includes peer observations are more likely to remain in the teaching profession beyond four years than other teachers (Odell & Ferraro, 1992).

Similarly, GTAs must observe a model class taught by their language coordinator and conduct peer observations for the methods class. But, many GTAs make additional visits to each other's classrooms on their own initiative. The department also invites them to observe regular faculty and provides them with a video library of teaching demonstrations by experienced teachers and GTAs.

Micro-teaching, like teacher observation, is a traditional element in teacher education. As early as 1969, Allen and Ryan prescribed micro-teaching for teacher education. At Kent, preservice K-12 teachers present numerous mini-lessons during their methods classes and self- and peer-critique their performances. While Allen and Ryan emphasize micro-teaching as practice teaching, we prefer to consider it protected teaching. Methods students teach their peers under the protection of the methods instructor, and they also teach mini-lessons in area K-12 school settings under the protection of a host teacher. GTAs teach in the model class under the protection of their language coordinator and with the support of other novice GTAs. For all three groups, micro-teaching is always a collaborative experience during which observing students learn new techniques and the micro-teacher receives formative feedback, thus developing professional confidence, effective teaching, and rapport (Wadlington, Partridge & Slaton, 1998).

Teacher reflection is defined as an approach that "seeks to cultivate . . . the kind of inquiring mind and critical attitude that will foster continued professional development throughout the career" (Joiner, 1993, p. 208). Reflection at Kent is encouraged through the development of portfolios and journals: one or both are required in preservice, GTA, and specialty methods classes in the M.A. program (e.g., Teaching Literature and Culture). Students and teachers collaborate in the planning of individual portfolios, which are recommended by numerous researchers, including

Boyer (1990, pp. 40-41), and Wade and Yarbrough (1996), whose student respondents reported that portfolio assignments caused them to reflect upon course content. Pleasants, Johnson, and Trent concluded from student responses that "the portfolio can function as an assessment tool that allows students to construct new knowledge, extend their thinking, and apply course content in personally meaningful and relevant ways" (1998, p. 54).

The use of a portfolio is only one way to encourage teacher reflection; another is the dialogue journal. Found to be useful in teacher education situations (e.g., Bacon, 1995; Stevenson & Jenkins, 1994; Wallace, 1999), dialogue journals enhance the collaborative relationship between preservice and inservice K-12 teachers or GTAs and their university instructors. Self-critiques of field experience teaching, methods class presentations, and student teaching continue the reflection necessary to professional development for teachers, empowering them to become more creative and effective, according to Singh, Doyle, Rose and Kennedy (1997).

Coordination and supervision might seem contrary to the conception of collaboration because they traditionally involve asymmetrical relationships of power and authority between the coordinator and the coordinated. Supervisory relationships vary, however. Kapuscinski (1997) identifies three types of relationships between cooperating teachers and interns: master-apprentice (intern is expected to learn from the master teacher), idiosyncratic (intern is expected to develop his/her own teaching style), and interdependent. In interdependent relationships, the ideal, according to Kapuscinski, both the intern and the cooperating teacher explore instructional strategies and reflect on their effectiveness together (p. 6). Dillenbourg suggests that a situation is more likely to be perceived as collaborative if the participants are status equals, but he also notes that perceptions of symmetry may be objective or subjective and are not static (1999, pp. 9-10). Thus, it is possible for teachers-in-training and supervisors or coordinators to collaborate, but efforts must be made to build and maintain trust, and coordinators must also benefit from the experience.

While it is true that the student teacher is in a supervised position with a cooperating teacher, school-based administrators, and university supervisors, he or she finds collaboration to be the norm at Kent where all parties operate as a team to assure the successful teaching experience of the student teacher. To further the collaborative nature of this experience, M.A. students who are practicing K-12 teachers sometimes serve as cooperating teachers for our preservice undergraduates. Also, former students who are first- and second-year teachers are invited to return to campus to share their experiences, offer suggestions, and provide support.

While the GTA/coordinator relationship has an asymmetrical structure, GTAs find coordinators to be supportive rather than authoritative, and evaluations tend to be formative rather than summative. Coordinators also benefit from the relationship: GTAs' suggestions have helped the graduate programs evolve to meet everyone's needs better.

University supervisors, K-12 cooperating teachers, inservice-teaching M.A. students and regular Kent faculty promote *socialization into the profession* for our preservice undergraduates through coursework, advising, mentoring, and teacher gatherings. Our new pro-active advising system ensures that B.A. language majors minoring in Education meet with their language pedagogy advisor every semester before registering. While the primary objective of these meetings is scheduling, advisors also discuss program options; encourage study abroad; and inform advisees of professional activities, opportunities, and scholarships. In their K-12 school settings, cooperating teachers encourage undergraduate student teachers to participate in extra-curricular experiences (e.g., school board meetings, language clubs, athletic events).

GTAs are socialized into their area of concentration (pedagogy, literature or translation) through their assistantships, which include research and teaching duties; by their coordinators, thesis advisors and other faculty; and by experienced GTAs. This year, GTAs established KentLingua, a student-generated organization designed to help them learn about career opportunities and to establish and maintain relationships between M.A. graduates and new GTAs.

Staton and Darling suggest that socialization to the GTA role "occurs through a process of communication" whereby they "develop a social support system, obtain information, adjust to rules and policies, and generate new ideas about teaching and research" (1989, pp. 17-18). We facilitate this process by creating opportunities for GTAs to socialize with peers and faculty at a fall social and during monthly gatherings of all GTAs and coordinators. New GTAs share offices and computer-laboratory space with experienced GTAs, an arrangement that promotes sharing of information and resources.

Pons (1993) recommends that GTAs participate in the department's undergraduate curriculum committee. At Kent, GTAs participate in and vote on not only the department's graduate/undergraduate curriculum committee but also on its graduate studies and language instruction committees.

An important activity for preservice and inservice teachers and GTAs is gathering with other professionals to discuss teaching issues. At Kent, preservice teachers, GTAs and other M.A. students, and area K-12 teachers are invited to attend teaching workshops led by guest speakers, satellite teleconferences, and teaching circles led by Kent faculty. Teaching workshops have focused on portfolio development, using legends to teach language, and authentic classroom discourse; teleconferences have featured the integration of technology into language teaching and the role of grammar in the communicative classroom; teaching circles (as promoted by Boyer, 1990, p. 30) have discussed the role of teacher talk, the use of visuals, and task-based instruction.

All three groups of teachers are also encouraged to network professionally by attending or presenting at Northeast Ohio Language Alliance (NEOLA) meetings and the annual conference of the Ohio Foreign Language Association (OFLA). NEOLA is one of many successful K-16 regional alliances, which Silber and Waterfall credit with building self-esteem and thereby "breaking us out of our isolation" (1988, p. 588). And, Riordan notes the "marvelous growth and good health" of the Academic Alliance project nationwide (1989, p. 186), a project that continues to be successful. Kent faculty also encourage presentations and participation by all three teachers' groups at the OFLA conference, where scholarships for university students are an added incentive to attend.

Collaboration between KSU and K-12 FL teachers continued in a new format during the summer of 2000 when a National Endowment for the Humanities/Ohio Humanities Council grant provided a five-day Foreign Language Teachers Institute for 35 FL teachers from all areas of Ohio. This Institute addressed the two most important inservice training topics, according to Wolf and Riordan (1991): oral proficiency and promoting and maintaining interest in language study. These researchers also identified the two most preferred forms of inservice activity: professional reading and collegial discussions, the primary means of knowledge-sharing at the Institute. Centered around the theme of Diversity in the Global Community, faculty-led panel discussions in English for all the Institute participants provided knowledge about the social, political, historical, and economic realities of the target cultures every morning. Then, participants practiced real-life language use at second language lunch tables. After lunch, academic language proficiency was addressed in French, German, and Spanish language sessions that focused on literature and culture, with special sessions on etymology, linguistics, and technology.

Instructional media supported many sessions at the Institute and enrich our collaborative undertakings. As previously noted, we have used video-tapes for micro-teaching, coordination and supervision, and for providing examples of model teaching. We have also scheduled several satellite tele-conferences for all three groups of teachers.

Computer technology in the form of e-mail, listservs, and bulletin boards has proven useful in promoting opportunities for collaboration. E-mail can be used as a means for disseminating instructional information and for en-hancing or replacing face-to-face interaction. Johanson, Norland, Olson, Huth, and Bodensteiner (1999) found that "listservs provide a rich forum for student teachers to flesh out their reflections on teaching, to touch bases with their colleagues and to seek (and give) advice" (1999, p. 3). Kirk (2000) has noted that preservice teachers who used a private chat room were more highly engaged in their collegial interactions and developed a strong class culture. According to Wu and Lee (1999), the unique text-based format of the electronic bulletin board encourages its users to "verbalize not only their beliefs and actions, but also the reasoning process." Bulletin board postings can be retained indefinitely, thus allowing users the opportunity to witness their growth and progress.

The use of computer-mediated collaboration varies according to users' needs. All members of the Pedagogy Unit use e-mail for rapid communica-tion, and they and their students are all encouraged to subscribe to professional listservs, such as FLTeach and NetTeach as well as the Kent-based FL pedagogy listserv. Additional listservs and bulletin boards are used by individual coordinators, supervisors, and instructors in the peda-gogy programs to problem-solve, discuss new ideas, and give immediate feedback on student teaching. In addition, Kent's GTAs, coordinators, and basic language course instructors share their teaching materials on a server accessible to all members of MCLS. All of these computer-enhanced col-laborations complement regularly scheduled and spontaneous face-to-face meetings.

Data Supporting Collaboration at Kent

Preservice teachers' survey

Preservice teachers recommended two improvements in teacher train-ing on a short answer survey: more time with cooperating teachers and more training with instructional technology. On Likert-scale questions (from 1 to 5, with 5 being most positive) they rated support from university pro-fessors at 4.5; from professional organizations at 4; from fellow student teachers in training at 4.75; and from cooperating teachers, family and friends at 4. It is noteworthy that support provided by fellow student teachers ranks the highest, most likely due to the deliberate encouragement of collaboration among student teachers in their courses and in multimedia fora.

M.A. graduates' survey

A survey of M.A. graduates within the past 5 years revealed general satisfaction with current programs in French, German, Latin, and Spanish (Pedagogy Concentration). Graduates offered their opinions of all courses in the program on a Likert-scale questionnaire (1 to 5, with 5 most positive). Courses where collaboration plays a key role were ranked more highly than all others (e.g., Teaching Literature and Culture, 4.67; Computers in Second Language Teaching, 4.67).

Collaboration between M.A. students and faculty becomes most intensive with final projects, when students share in the preparation of their papers, and even faculty who are not committee members advise the M.A. candidates. Recent papers include detailed curriculum proposals and survey, experimental, and qualitative research projects during which students may work collaboratively with KSU faculty members, K-12 teachers and students, or MCLS undergraduates.

GTA survey

Comments from GTAs on student evaluations for their methods class clearly indicate that this class encourages collaboration, sharing of ideas, and dialogue about teaching issues. When asked what aspects of the course were especially successful, students answered that "The instructor ... facilitated the exchange of ideas in class" and allowed "Grads to workshop together, i.e., sharing teaching ideas and issues." Another comment was: "I thoroughly enjoyed it as a forum for pedagogic discussion."

A GTA survey on sharing materials and ideas revealed the following data, based on 1 as never, 2 as almost never, 3 as 1-2 times per week, and 4 as frequently. GTAs responded to: "How often do you (a) get teaching ideas or materials from other GTAs? (mean response = 2.83); (b) get ideas from observing the model instructor/class? (mean = 3.25); (c) get ideas from weekly meetings with the coordinator? (mean = 3.25); (d) share your ideas and materials with other GTAs? (mean = 3.08); and (e) talk about teaching problems and solutions with other GTAs? (mean = 3.42). Clearly, the GTAs share teaching problems and solutions among themselves, but they get ideas mostly from the coordinator, who also teaches the model class. Comments corroborated this: "Coordinators, professors and instructors are always available to help," and "Coming to see [the coordinator] regularly at her office generated discussion about our teaching."

Conclusions and Recommendations

Founded as a normal, or teacher training school in 1910, Kent State University is a comprehensive institution with "teacher training roots" (Boyer, p. 63) where the scholarship of teaching is becoming a top priority. Interaction among our three constituencies continues this Kent tradition. Preservice teachers benefit from the presence of international and domestic GTAs; inservice K-12 teachers who are M.A. students serve as cooperative teachers for methods class field experiences and student teaching and often attend class with both preservice teachers and GTAs. Collaboration among these groups is pervasive and productive.

In reference to FL alliances, Silber and Waterfall assert that because of their collaborative, "We are a team now" (1988, p. 589). It is in this spirit that the teacher education programs at Kent thrive. We strive for the "ideal educational scenario" (Trentin, 1999, p. 148) where students, teachers, and experts all collaborate.

While the examples of collaboration described above have served us well, we would not argue that they are appropriate for all situations. Rather, we would suggest that others examine and, perhaps, choose one or more of our strategies in their own pursuit of collaboration in teacher training.

Based on our experience with preservice and inservice K-12 teachers and GTAs, the Pedagogy Unit faculty at Kent recommend the following:

- Use classroom observations to share methodological knowledge and promote critical judgment.
- Encourage micro-teaching in a non-threatening, protected environment, and record lessons on videotape.
- Promote teacher reflection with professional portfolios, dialogue journals, and electronic bulletin boards.
- Foster an atmosphere of mutual support and learning within supervisory relationships.
- Encourage participation in teacher gatherings to promote knowledge dissemination and collegiality.

- Use modern media to enhance all aspects of teacher education programs, including resource sharing and communication by e-mail, listservs, and bulletin boards among preservice and inservice teachers, GTAs, cooperating teachers, university-based supervisors and faculty and program coordinators.

Though our experiences are perhaps unique, it is our hope that other institutions may find these suggestions useful and adaptable for their own needs in foreign and second language teacher education.

References

Allen, D., & Ryan, K. (1969). *Microteaching.* Reading, MA: Addison-Wesley.

American Council on the Teaching of Foreign Languages. (1988). ACTFL provisional program guidelines for foreign language teacher education. *Foreign Language Annals, 21,* 71-82.

Bacon, S. (1995). Coming to grips with the culture: Another use of dialogue journals in teacher education. *Foreign Language Annals, 28,* 193-207.

Boehrer, J. & Sarkisian, E. (1985). The teaching assistant's point of view. In J. D. W. Andrews (Ed.), *Strengthening the teaching assistant faculty* (pp. 7-20). San Francisco: Jossey-Bass.

Boyer, E. L. (1990). *Scholarship reconsidered: Priorities of the professoriate.* San Francisco: Jossey-Bass.

Christiansen, L., Goulet, L., Krentz, C., & Maeers, M. (Eds.). (1997). *Recreating relationships: Collaboration and educational reform* (pp. xv-xviii). New York: SUNY Press.

Diamond, R. M. & Gray, P. J. (1998). *1997 National study of teaching assistants.* Syracuse, NY: Center for Instructional Development, Syracuse University.

Dillenbourg, P. (1999). Introduction: What do you mean by "collaborative learning"? In P. Dillenbourg (Ed.), *Collaborative learning: Cognitive and computational approaches* (pp. 1-19). Amsterdam: Pergamon.

Educational Testing Service. (1995). *Pathwise classroom observation system.* Princeton, NJ: Educational Testing Service.

Friesen, D. (1997). The meaning of collaboration: Redefining pedagogical relationships in student teaching. In L. Christiansen, L. Goulet, C. Krentz, & M. Maeers (Eds.), *Recreating relationships: Collaboration and educational reform* (pp. 219-231). New York: SUNY Press.

Holmes Group. (1986). *Tomorrow's teachers: A report of the Holmes Group.* East Lansing, MI: The Holmes Group.

Johanson, R. P., Norland, D. L., Olson, E., Huth, L., & Bodensteiner, R. (1999). Internet and list-serves to support the student teaching semester. Paper presented at the Annual Meeting of the American Association of Colleges for Teacher Education, Washington. (ERIC Document Reproduction Service No. ED 428060).

Joiner, E. G. (1993). Reflecting on teacher development. In G. Guntermann (Ed.), *Developing language teachers for a changing world* (pp. 187-212). Lincolnwood, IL: National Textbook Company.

Kapuscinski, P. (1997). The collaborative lens: A new look at an old research study. In L. Christiansen, L. Goulet, C. Krentz, & M. Maeers (Eds.), *Recreating relationships: Collaboration and educational reform* (pp. 219-231). New York: SUNY Press.

Kirk, R. (2000). A study of the use of a private chat room to increase reflective thinking in pre-service teachers. *College Student Journal, 34,* 115-122.

Lee, J. F. (1989). *A manual and practical guide to directing foreign language programs and training graduate teaching assistants.* Boston: McGraw-Hill.

Lee, J. F. & VanPatten, B. (1995). *Making communicative language teaching happen.* New York: McGraw-Hill.

Manley, J. H., Smith, S., McMinn, J. T., & Prévost, M. A. (1998). *Horizons.* Boston: Heinle & Heinle.

National Standards in Foreign Language Education Project. (1996). *Standards for foreign language learning: Preparing for the 21st century.* Lawrence, KS: Allen Press, Inc.

Nerenz, A. G., Herron, C. A., & Knop, C. K. (1979). The training of graduate teaching assistants in foreign languages: A review of literature and description of contemporary programs. *French Review, 52,* 873-888.

Nicholls, G. (1997). *Collaborative change in education.* London: Kogan Page.

Odell, S. & Ferraro, D. (1992). Teacher mentoring and teacher retention. *Journal of Teacher Education, 43,* 200-204.

Olson, G. (1990). The nature of collaboration. In H. Schwartz (Ed.), *Collaboration: Building common agendas* (pp. 11-15). (Teacher education monograph No. 10). Washington: ERIC Clearinghouse on Teacher Education.

Pleasants, H.M., Johnson, C.B., & Trent, S.C. (1998). Reflecting, reconceptualizing, and revising: The evolution of a portfolio assignment in a multicultural teacher education course. *Remedial and Special Education, 19,* 46-58.

Pons, C. R. (1993). TA supervision: Are we preparing a future professoriate? In D. P. Benseler (Ed.), *The dynamics of language program direction* (pp. 19-31). Boston: Heinle & Heinle.

Riordan, K. M. (1989). Teachers teaching teachers: An inservice model that works. *Foreign Language Annals, 22,* 185-188.

Schwartz, H. (Ed.) (1990). *Collaboration: Building common agendas.* (Teacher Education Monograph No. 10). Washington: ERIC Clearinghouse on Teacher Education.

Shaw, R. (1995). *Teacher training in secondary schools.* London: Kogan Page.

Silber, W. & Waterfall, B. (1988). Academic alliances: School/college faculty collaboratives. *Foreign Languages Annals 21,* 587-590.

Singh, A., Doyle, C., Rose, A., & Kennedy, W. (1997). Reflective internship and the phobia of classroom management. *Australian Journal of Education, 41,* 105-118.

Staton, A. Q. & Darling, A. L. (1989). Socialization of teaching assistants. In J. D. Nyquist, R. D. Abbott, & D. H. Wulff (Eds.), *Teaching assistant training in the 1990s* (pp. 15-23). San Francisco: Jossey-Bass, Inc.

Stevenson, J. L. & Jenkins, S. (1994). Journal writing in the training of international teaching assistants. *Journal of Second Language Writing 3,* 97-120.

Struyk, L. R., Cole, K. B., & Kinder, D. (1995). Utilizing multimedia applications to enhance instruction of performance assessment for preservice teachers. *Journal of Educational Computing Research, 13,* 227-36.

Struyk, L. R. & McCoy, L. H. (1993). Pre-service teachers' use of videotape for self-evaluation. *The Clearing House, 67,* 31-34.

Trentin, G. (1999). Network-based collaborative education. *International Journal of Instructional Media, 26,* 145-57.

Wade, R. C., & Yarbrough, D. B. (1996). Portfolios: A tool for reflective thinking in teacher education? *Teaching and Teacher Education, 12,* 63-79.

Wadlington, E., Partridge, M. E., & Slaton, E. (1998). Alleviating stress in pre-service teachers during field experiences. *Education 119,* 335-348.

Wallace, J. (1999). Dialogue journals. In P. Graham, S. Hudson-Ross, C. Adkins, P. McWhorter, & J. M. Stewart (Eds.), *Teacher mentor: A dialogue for collaborative learning* (pp. 34-45). New York: Teachers College Press, Columbia University.

Wing, B. H. (1993). The Pedagogical imperative in foreign language teacher education. In G. Guntermann (Ed.), *Developing language teachers for a changing world* (pp. 159-186). Lincolnwood, IL: National Textbook Company.

Wolf, W. C., Jr. & Riordan, K. M. (1991). Foreign language teachers' demographic characteristics, inservice training needs, and attitudes toward teaching. *Foreign Language Annals, 24,* 471-478.

Worthen, T. K. (1992). The frustrated GTA: A qualitative investigation identifying the needs within the graduate teaching assistant experience. Paper presented at the Annual Meeting of the Speech Communication Association, Chicago. (ERIC Document Reproduction Service No. ED 355598).

Wu, C-C, & Lee, G. C. (1999). Use of BBS to facilitate a teaching practicum course. *Computers and Education, 32,* 239-247.

2
Dangerous Assumptions in Early Language Learning Programs

Helena Curtain
University of Wisconsin-Milwaukee

Carol Ann Pesola Dahlberg
Concordia College

The United States has been experiencing a resurgence of interest in language education, especially at the elementary school level. Good news regarding the status of early language learning has emerged from a survey (Branaman and Rhodes, 1998) that provides valuable information about the status of languages in the USA. In addition to the survey, the Center for Applied Linguistics has also established a partial directory of early language learning programs (www.cal.org) in which over 3,000 programs are listed.

In the United States, approximately 52% of high school students (usually grades 9-12), 36% of middle school students (usually Grades 5-8 or Grades 6-8), and 31 % of elementary school students (usually Grades Kindergarten through 5 or 6) receive foreign language instruction. In 1997, over four million elementary school students (out of 27.1 million) were enrolled in foreign language classes across the country. Of these, more than two-and-a-half million students were in public schools and one-and-a-half million in private schools. In the public elementary schools that taught foreign language, approximately half the students were provided foreign language instruction. According to Branaman and Rhodes (1998), foreign language instruction in elementary schools has increased by nearly 10% during the past decade. In 1987, just over one in five (22%) elementary schools reported teaching foreign languages; by 1997 the percentage had risen to 31% (approximately one in three), a statistically significant increase. The percentage of secondary schools teaching foreign language remained fairly stable (87% in 1987 and 86% in 1997). Among the one-third of elementary schools that offered foreign language study, the majority (79%) provided programs aimed at various kinds of introductory exposure to the language, while 21% offered programs having overall proficiency as one of the goals. These data mean that only 7% of all elementary schools (increased from 3% in 1987) offered instruction in which the students were likely to attain a high level of fluency, as recommended in the goals of the national standards (1996).

Many of the new language programs that abound at the elementary school level have been established in compliance with recent state mandates. Others were developed in response to parental pressure for early language learning opportunities for their children. The growing body of information about cognitive and academic benefits of early bilingualism has no doubt added to the continued development and expansion of these programs. Unfortunately, only a few of these programs are likely to succeed over an extended period of time. Many others risk failure because of decisions based on faulty assumptions about foreign language learning, language programs, curriculum, teachers, and young language learners. Some of these faulty assumptions are examined in this article and are identified at the beginning of each section.

"A little bit of language is better than no language at all."
"Children's language learning is a magical process unrelated to the amount of time allocated to the task."

These assumptions lead to the dangerous belief that any amount of time allocated to an elementary school program will result in the promised outcomes. While much has been written about the ease and naturalness with which young children can learn other languages, children cannot learn language if they are not sufficiently exposed to it.

There are many varieties of early foreign language programs currently being offered in the United States. Some programs that label themselves "FLES" (foreign language in the elementary school), offer instruction in a foreign language once a week for 20 minutes. Others may offer instruction three times a week for 30 minutes, while still others offer it every day for 45 minutes. Some programs begin language instruction as early as Kindergarten, whereas others may not start until Grade 4 or 5. A number of programs continue through Grade 8; others are offered only in the elementary school.

There is a widespread belief that giving all children a little bit of language is an effective way to implement an early language learning program. In effect, this belief holds that it does not really matter how much time is allocated for language instruction as long as children have some exposure. This assumption is in direct contradiction to the fact that in order to achieve language fluency an extended sequence of instruction and a certain amount of time are needed. Various experts have attempted to pinpoint the time issue. Curtain and Pesola (1994) have recommended that a minimum time allotment for Foreign Language in the Elementary School (FLES) programs should be 30 minutes three times per week. A national group of experts that convened to try to achieve consensus on the time issue (Rosenbusch, 1992) recommended a slightly smaller amount of time and agreed that classes should meet all year within the school day (at least every other day), for a minimum average of 75 minutes per week. Despite the fact that both of these minimum recommendations are very low, there are many programs that do not meet even these minimum time allocations.

In regard to the belief that a little bit of language is better than no language, Frank Grittner (1991), relating an account of visiting a program in which there were only 24 hours of contact time in a year, criticizes the practice of implementing programs with very little time devoted to language learning:

> Twenty-four hours per year–the equivalent of a few days' visit to a Spanish-speaking country! A total of seventy-two hours, over a three-year period! And according to government estimates, it takes eight times that (600 hours) to bring well-motivated adults to the point where they can "satisfy basic survival needs and meet minimum courtesy requirements in Spanish." Clearly, the expectations of these FLES programs were totally unreasonable simply in terms of the allocated time provided. We should not have implied that fluency would result (p.183).

In a study conducted by Curtain (1998), teachers were consistent in their remarks about the need for more time. If more time were provided for early language learning, the students would not have to start over just when the "flow gets going" and they would not "forget from one day to the next." With more time, students would be able to practice language as a whole class as well as on a group and individual basis and be able to "do something meaningful with the language." Students would be able to "produce more language and feel confident in their abilities." "With longer time, students would have opportunity for reflection and would be able to synthesize and produce language." The most telling comment was from one teacher who stated: "With only two days per week, students get tired of language. They see a lot of the same things, don't seem to progress. A low percentage of students are opting to go on in eighth grade."

"Early language learning teachers can work in any conditions."

There are dangers in the proliferation of early language learning programs without attention to the many stress factors involved in typical teacher work loads. Teachers are often expected to teach upward of 200 and as many as 500 plus students; they are also expected to teach 10-14 classes per day. (The maximum we would recommend is eight.) They are often asked to develop curriculum since there are few appropriate commercial materials available for elementary school languages. As a result, it is often hard to maintain staff in such demanding programs. It is not physically possible to sustain such a load over a period of time. If teachers work in hostile conditions, they will burn out, leave the profession, or they will opt for regular classrooms. It is imperative that we build programs that are good for children and good for teachers.

Teacher workloads and stress factors at this level often include:

- responsibilities for creating a curriculum framework and for writing daily curriculum activities while teaching at the same time;
- numerous instructional groups–sometimes as many as 14 classes taught in a day;
- numbers of students–sometimes as many as 600 in a week;
- back-to-back scheduling so there is no time between classes;
- traveling between buildings, sometimes three buildings in a day;
- traveling from classroom to classroom with materials and lessons on a cart;
- working within other teachers' classroom environments and the different emotional climate of each classroom;
- having to teach many levels in a day–jumping from Kindergarten to Grade 5 to Grade 2 in one day;
- lack of professional support (i.e., program coordinator) and in-service appropriate to the needs of language teachers;
- lack of time to collaborate with grade level classroom teachers;
- lack of time to collaborate with other teachers in the K-12 sequence;
- lack of appropriate materials; and
- perception that the language teacher need have the same number of contact minutes as regular classroom teachers and other specialist staff members in order to represent an equitable load.

"There is an obvious language choice for an elementary school language program."

This assumption challenges the tradition, long held in this country, of offering a variety of languages because it is impossible to predict which language will be the one needed by students in the future. Met (1989) makes a case for offering a variety of languages, citing the multiethnic society in which we live, and the economic and political need for U.S. citizens who speak many different languages. Only through participation in a long sequence of language study, beginning in the elementary school, can real fluency develop before students enter the working world.

Children are natural language learners, and languages perceived by adults as "difficult" can be offered with great success as early as Pre-Kindergarten. Early experience with a language also makes it easier for a learner to acquire a third and even a fourth language at a later point in life. If a single language is chosen at the elementary school level, it is highly recommended that additional languages be made available at later levels, along with the option of continuing the language begun in elementary school. When FLES programs are implemented, the need to insure the survival of other languages must be taken into account.

"Language classes should be treated differently from other parts of the curriculum in terms of assessment, grading, and reporting."

It is important to note that in all other industrialized nations, languages have status as academic subjects and are a part of the core curriculum of every school, usually starting by Grade 5 at the latest. We must convince our academic leaders that language learning is on a par with every other elementary school subject.

One way to underscore the academic nature of language programs is to bring assessment and grading practices in language programs into line with those in other academic areas of the elementary school. Some elementary school language teachers have expressed reluctance to provide regular assessments and grading, fearing that motivation and feelings of success on the part of children will be negatively affected. A number of successful, well-established programs, however, have developed successful assessment and grading practices that acknowledge and document the success of the students and the program. Seven excellent examples are found in a recently-published book by Gilzow and Branahan, *Lessons Learned: Model Early Foreign Language Programs* (2000).

"Teachers possessing less language proficiency should teach lower grade levels."

It requires the same level of language skill to teach younger learners as to teach older learners–in fact, even greater skills may be necessary. Elementary school foreign language teachers usually need to develop and translate basic and supplementary materials, as well as deliver them in the target language. While systematic grammar instruction may not be an explicit part of the elementary school program, the effective teacher embeds and develops grammatical concepts and practice in every part of the curriculum. Part of the effectiveness of an early language program comes from the technique of surrounding learners with the new language in every aspect of classroom life, a strategy that requires real linguistic fluency and flexibility. Especially in the case of content-related instruction, in which connections are made to the general curriculum of the elementary school, the teacher needs to be able to adapt, explain, and contextualize new concepts and information in the target language. All of these activities require a sophisticated ability to use and analyze language, especially at lower grade levels.

"A native speaker is always a better choice as a language teacher than someone who has learned the language in order to teach it."

This assumption may lead to programs staffed by teachers who have no experience teaching languages, and perhaps no experience teaching children.

It has been the experience of a number of programs that inexperienced native speakers of the language have had a difficult time relating to American children and are not prepared to deal with the many challenges of the elementary school foreign language program. The teacher who has learned the target language in order to teach it sometimes has an awareness of the obstacles faced by the learner that the native speaker lacks.

There is no question that the quality of the language skills developed by children in an elementary school program is related to the language skills of the teacher. Every elementary school language teacher should be a fluent speaker of the language, as well as a skilled and well-prepared teacher of children. Both qualities are necessary in order to have the best possible teacher of the language, and neither characteristic can fully compensate for the lack of the other.

"Time devoted to learning a new language deprives children of needed time in essential content areas."

The topics treated in a well-conceived language learning program relate to the world of the child. These topics or contexts can vary greatly from those (1) based on the regular school curriculum (i.e., content-based or content-related instruction) to those (2) more typically found in early language learning programs (i.e., drama, role-play, games, songs, children's literature, folk and fairy tales, storytelling and puppetry). All of these topics contribute to the other curricular content areas and to the basic mission of the school because they all enhance children's learning.

Planning language instruction that connects to the regular school curriculum is an important component of a well-conceived early language learning program. Sometimes an attempt to satisfy this goal is pursued in content-based or content-related instruction, meaning that a specific portion of the regular school curriculum is taught through the new language. This ill-conceived approach is based on an idea that the promise of delivering specific subject area content in the language will diffuse the objection that we are taking time away from the regular curriculum. This assumption maintains that language instruction in FLES programs can be solely delivered in specific content areas such as science or social studies, much like language immersion programs. However, this approach is not appropriate for a FLES program since it deprives students of a well-rounded language curriculum with contexts for many kinds of language expression.

Conclusion

Many of the problems that plague us today were also prevalent in the 1960s, when there was a short-lived proliferation of early language learning programs. The problems that have been addressed in this paper are very similar to those of 40 years ago: a shortage of qualified teachers, a tendency to establish programs without sufficient planning or careful selection of teachers and materials, a lack of clarity about the connection between program goals and the amount of time allocated to the program, and a willingness to promise whatever the public wants to hear. Many of the reasons for this short period of popularity are described in "A Survey of FLES Practices," a report written for the Modern Language Association in 1961. After visiting 62 communities with reportedly good FLES programs in the spring of 1961, Alkonis and Brophy drew the following conclusions (pp. 213-217):

1. A majority of the FLES programs that we observed do not fulfill the primary aim of such a program–teaching the four language skills–even when this is clearly stated as their objective. Sometimes the teacher is weak; just as often the weakness lies beyond the teacher's control, in the materials or the scheduling.

2. Many programs emphasized such aims as "world understanding" or "broadened horizons" to the extent that it is a clear misnomer to call them *language* programs. We saw no evidence of effective evaluation of the teaching directed toward these objectives....

3. There is such a diversity of linguistic content that a general evaluation of results using a single test or series of tests appears to be impracticable.

4. From the widespread emphasis upon learning lists of words, we conclude that a majority of the FLES teachers think of language as words to be learned in isolation and then strung into "conversation." They showed no awareness of the interacting systems of structure or patterns that are basic to each language.

5. Many programs, started without planning and provision for the materials, the instruction, and the eventual integration with junior- and senior-high school courses, are considered "experimental," but there is no clear statement of the conditions and terms of the experiment and no provision for an evaluation of its results.

6. The most obvious weakness is lack of teachers with sufficient skill in the language and training in methods. (This is no reflection on the sincerity, the enthusiasm, or the good will of the instructors. How many of us, with no knowledge of music and unable to play the piano, could successfully teach a music class?)

7. In many schools–certainly in the majority of those we visited–FLES is conceived of as merely a preview or prelude to "real" language learning (which will begin in the high school) rather than as a serious, systematic attempt to develop attitudes and skills.

8. Few programs are planned as an unbroken, cumulative sequence from the primary through the junior high school, partly because of the lack of appropriate teaching materials for the junior high school, but more because of the inadequacy of the FLES work itself.

The eight observations made by Alkonis and Brophy effectively summarized the problems that most FLES programs of the 1960s failed to resolve. As budgets tightened and priorities shifted, as promised results failed to materialize, as graduates of FLES programs failed to meet the expectations of junior and senior high teachers, language programs in the elementary school lost their credibility as well as their value as a status symbol. These programs were among the first to be cut when school systems evaluated their curricula to make room for new trends and emphases. We cannot let this happen again! We must do our best to make sure that the assumptions mentioned here are corrected!

References

Alkonis, N. V., & Brophy, M. (1961). A Survey of FLES Practices. *Reports of surveys and studies in the teaching of modern foreign languages, 1959-1961*. New York: The Modern Language Association of America.

Branaman, L., & Rhodes, N. (1998). *A national survey of foreign language instruction in elementary and secondary schools*. Washington, D.C.: U.S. Department of Education, Office of Postsecondary Education, International Research and Studies Programs, Center for Applied Linguistics.

Curtain, H. (1998). Effects of elementary school foreign language program models on foreign language proficiency. Unpublished doctoral dissertation. University of Wisconsin-Milwaukee.

Curtain, H., & Pesola, C. A. (1994). *Languages and children: Making the match*. (2nd Ed.) Glenview, IL: Scott-Foresman.

Gilzow, D. F.& Branaman, L. E. (2000). *Lessons learned: Model early foreign language programs*. McHenry, IL: Delta Systems Co., Inc.

Grittner, F. (1991). Foreign languages for children: Let's do it right this time. *Hispania, 74*(1), (March, 1991), 182-186.

Met, M. (1989). Which foreign languages should students learn? *Educational Leadership, 47*(1), 54-58.

National Standards in Foreign Language Education Project. (1996). *Standards for foreign language learning: Preparing for the 21st century*. Lawrence, KS: Allen Press.

Rosenbusch, M. (Ed.). (1992*). Colloquium on foreign languages in the elementary school curriculum*. New York: Goethe House.

3
IN-VISION: An Innovative Model for K-12 Spanish in Rural Schools

Marie Trayer
IN-VISION Technology Challenge Project

Introduction

Many of the nation's communities realize the importance of a K-12 articulated foreign language program in their schools, and often-cited studies emphasize the advantages of starting young children in foreign language instruction. However, implementing these programs is difficult for a variety of reasons. One of the most notable is the shortage of certified foreign language teachers at all levels faced by schools across the country. Added to the teacher shortage are budgetary limitations; district personnel interested in K-12 programs cite the financial drain of hiring more teachers. It is no surprise that rural schools are particularly disadvantaged because of long distances that isolate them from rich language resources and opportunities. However, the *IN-VISION* model overcomes the challenges of teacher shortages, distance, and costly expenditures. A federal technology challenge grant, *IN-VISION* provides 14 Iowa and Nebraska rural schools with a K-12 Spanish program. The model emphasizes foreign language instruction, supported by computer and telecommunication technologies, as a way to reinforce the core curriculum in both the elementary and secondary levels.

K-12 Spanish Program

The K-12 Spanish language program incorporates several interwoven elements: classroom teachers learning Spanish, the use of local native speaker Language Associates, the use of Language/Culture Assistants from Spain, the integration of Spanish with other disciplines, and the incorporation of technology. The Spanish lessons begin in the elementary school and move into the secondary school as additional grade levels are added annually. In the elementary classes, the Language Associate and classroom teacher work as a team, providing hands-on, communication-based Spanish instruction once or twice a week for 20 to 30 minutes. On the secondary level, *IN-VISION* supports the development of the project schools' articulated K-12 foreign language programs. Each project school has defined the secondary experience in a different way, so school staff members adjust schedules and personnel to assure continuous language learning at the middle school and high school levels.

Classroom Teachers

The elementary teachers' role in the model includes showing a weekly episode from the video series, *Español para Ti,*[1] incorporating Spanish into the core curriculum, reinforcing the vocabulary, and assisting the Language Associates with the activities and curriculum of the Spanish lessons. Students use Spanish software for supplementary practice and participate in other technology-based activities that the classroom teachers incorporate into the day's activities.

To fulfill this role, elementary teachers receive training in foreign language pedagogy, the use of technology in the classroom, Spanish language, and Hispanic cultures by attending Summer Institutes, as well as twice-monthly sessions via distance learning and on-site technology training sessions during the school year. After two years of participation, teachers travel to Costa Rica, where they attend a Spanish language institute while living with a family.

The four-day Summer Institutes, planned by a representative group of *IN-VISION* project teachers, provide classroom teachers with intensive Spanish and culture lessons. Summer Institute instructors are certified Spanish teachers and native speakers, many of whom are from participant *IN-VISION* project schools. These same instructors facilitate the distance learning sessions during the school year. The Summer Institutes feature small group and hands-on activities that have participants actively involved in learning.

Language Associates

The role of the native-speaking Language Associates is vital to the model. The qualifications that *IN-VISION* staff members require for native-speaking associates include experience working with children and an ability to learn and apply instructional concepts.

To foster the development of essential strategies necessary for successful language instruction, the Language Associates engage in modeling activities and team teaching with certified teachers hired to teach Spanish at the Summer Institutes. During the school year, *IN-VISION* staff members organize monthly in-service meetings and on-site coaching to further support the Language Associates' effectiveness in the classroom.

Language/Culture Assistants

A new program through the Embassy of Spain provides Language/ Culture Assistants. These native speakers, recent graduates from Spanish universities majoring in education, seek experience in U.S. schools teaching a language. The Assistants work 20 hours per week, are encouraged to take classes, and receive a stipend from the Embassy to defray expenses other than transportation and lodging, provided by the host school. *IN-VISION* has had three assistants who have been project Language Associates. They have been a welcome addition by contributing language and cultural background plus skills in pedagogy.

Curriculum

The curriculum for the elementary program is a composite of formats from numerous sources, with a standards-based K-6 curriculum as the foundation. The *IN-VISION* staff brought together a cadre of elementary classroom teachers, secondary Spanish teachers, K-6 elementary Spanish teachers, and Language Associates to write the curriculum, using the *Standards for Foreign Language Learning* (1996) and the *Nebraska Foreign Language Frameworks* (1996) as a foundation, and to design assessments that are standards-aligned. The aim of the *IN-VISION* curriculum is for students to be able to communicate meaningfully.

On-going contributions to the curriculum plan are provided by classroom teachers, who suggest themes and topics related to the core curriculum. This regular input reassures the classroom teachers that the Spanish lessons are not taking away instructional time from the core subjects but are, in fact, reinforcing basic content. The teachers are asked to complete a form for the Language Associates a week prior to the actual planned instruction, describing the content and recommending suggestions for integration into the Spanish lesson.

A third source for the curriculum is the video series *Español para Ti.* Classroom teachers facilitate practice of the previously learned vocabulary, show the video, and reinforce new vocabulary weekly by using one of the suggested activities from the video resource manual. Language Associates also support the new vocabulary through their Spanish lessons.

Special events and holidays that provide rich cultural experiences also play an important curricular role. *IN-VISION* schools celebrate the many Hispanic holidays within the classroom as well as throughout the school and community. Assemblies, Fiesta Days/Nights, and week-long celebrations provide rewarding opportunities for students, teachers, parents, and community members to raise their cultural awareness.

Some of the curricular models at the secondary level include a rotation of language instruction in the core subject area classrooms on a weekly basis. Another design relies strongly on integrating Spanish into the core curriculum. Secondary teams from *IN-VISION* schools have received training in writing integrated curricular units that incorporate Spanish into other disciplines and are implemented throughout the school year. Many of the secondary team members also attend the Spanish language and culture lessons presented during the Summer Institutes and via distance learning during the school year.

Evaluation

Results from an *IN-VISION* project evaluation suggest that the amount of time *IN-VISION* students participate in Spanish language instruction is the same as that of a typical FLES program. Certainly, the *IN-VISION* project's blending of multiple sources of instruction, plus the added facet of classroom teachers learning Spanish concurrently with their students, positively affects the richness and depth of student proficiency. The final program evaluation and analysis will be completed and reported at the end of the grant period.

Technology Integration

Teacher Training and Applications

IN-VISION provides extensive technology training for project teachers. During the Summer Institutes and on-site sessions throughout the school year, teachers learn how to incorporate key pals, multimedia presentations, and web-page design into their instruction, as well as become familiar with strategies for effective Internet use.

One of the training components requires teachers to write a technology-enhanced thematic plan (Grades K-3) or *WebQuest* (Grades 4-12) and implement the plan during the school year. These activities insure that student learning is enhanced by the technology applications. *IN-VISION* classrooms receive computers and software so that students will have easy access to the technologies.

IN-VISION has adopted another component of teacher technology training entitled *Gen wwwY*, designed by a Washington-based technology challenge grant project. This model includes the preparation of students in technology skills as well as social and adult-training skills. Students pair up with teachers to develop instructional units, teachers providing instructional expertise and students supplying the technology background.

Student Technology Applications

Student technology products and activities are varied. Examples of student work include: (1) the creation of books produced by digital cameras; (2) word processing applications of writing activities, such as a narrative description of students' school days; and (3) Internet projects such as the migration of the monarch butterflies and *MayaQuest*. Other uses of technology integrated into Spanish instruction include: (1) key pal exchanges among project schools as well as internationally, providing students with real contexts for writing Spanish; (2) web-based practice links on the *IN-VISION* web site as a supplement to in-class instruction; and (3) web pages co-created by students and teachers, featuring their own classroom or their school.

Another application of technology, encompassing an even broader spectrum of management, is video conferencing, which provides a rich, new mode for communicating with other students and with native speakers, facilitated by *Net Meeting* or *iVisit*, downloaded free off the Internet. The equipment requirements include a Web Cam, software to run the Web Cam, speakers, and a microphone. Although locating students in other countries who have the technology and schedules to accomplish real-time communication presents a challenge, within the U.S. there are many potential sites for K-12 student connections via video conferencing. Schools with native Spanish-speaking children can connect with schools where children have not had the opportunity to interact with many Hispanics.

IN-VISION staff members are experimenting with video conferencing as a means to connect native-speaking Language Associates to rural elementary schools. Using computers hooked up to the Internet and wired to projection devices, children can sit in their classrooms and interact with native speakers. Among the elements for the success of video conferencing, as an effective and innovative model for integrating technology into language instruction, is the essential inclusion of classroom teachers as equal and active participants in the planning and implementation of the lessons incorporating video conferencing.

Future Implementation of the Model in New Schools

IN-VISION has created three models for future implementation of the elementary program: Premium–The classroom teacher learns Spanish and partners with the Language Associate who visits the classrooms; Standard– the Language Associate visits the classroom; Basic–the Language Associate visits the classroom via video conferencing. All three models require training in instructional strategies for the Language Associate, and consultations by project staff insure the successful start-up for the elementary program. Materials prepared by *IN-VISION* supplement the lessons: *Resource Book for K-6 Spanish* (visuals, vocabulary, units), *Integrated Activities* (classroom activities for integrating Spanish into the content areas), *Idea Book* (K-6 activities), and *Technology Integration* (ideas for integrating technology into the elementary classroom).

Conclusion

The innovative combination of elements for the *IN-VISION* K-12 Spanish program provides a rich environment for students to make connections with the core curriculum while applying their new learning of Spanish in a variety of ways. The upcoming years will certainly be filled with expectancy as the profession and local schools explore avenues for providing extended sequences of foreign language instruction. The *IN-VISION* model provides an effective K-12 option for consideration, one that significantly reduces the challenges of cost, teacher shortage, and distance.

Notes

[1]   Distributed by National Textbook Company

References

National Standards in Foreign Language Education Project. (1996). *Standards for foreign language learning: Preparing for the 21st century*. Lawrence, KS: Allen Press.

Nebraska Department of Education. (1996). *Challenge for a new era: Nebraska K-12 foreign language frameworks*. Lincoln, NE: Nebraska Department of Education and the U.S. Department of Education's "Innovations in Education Grant."

4

Standards-Based Foreign Language Learning and Teachers' Pedagogical Beliefs

Linda Quinn Allen
Iowa State University

Many of today's foreign language programs are adapting their curricula to be more consistent with the *Standards for Foreign Language Learning* (1996, 1999). However, changing the curricula to reflect the standards does not necessarily mean that teachers can or will modify what they actually do in the classroom. If the standards are to achieve their potential impact, preparation of new teachers in standards-based foreign language learning and professional development for experienced teachers are crucial (Leighton & Sykes, 1992; Sparks, 1994; Wagner, 1993; cited in Glisan, 1996; National Standards in Foreign Language Education Project, 1996, p. 15). The literature suggests that professional development that provides teachers with a knowledge of the standards is not enough to stimulate a change in pedagogical practices. In order to effect change, professional development must engage teachers in the identification and clarification of their own beliefs about teaching and learning (Bailey et al., 1996; Anderson, 1995; Little, 1993).

During summers 1999 and 2000, I offered a graduate level course, entitled Standards-Based Foreign Language Instruction, for experienced foreign language teachers. The first and the last activities of the course were for participants to respond to the Foreign Language Education Questionnaire (FLEQ). This paper suggests that the FLEQ may be a means for stimulating an identification and consideration of teachers' own pedagogical beliefs about teaching and learning a foreign language. This paper describes the development of the FLEQ, presents a summary of the class participants' responses, and provides suggestions for future professional development and research.

Background

Each of us, as foreign language educators, has a personal theory about language learning and teaching. We all have beliefs about how learner variables– motivation, age, attitude, aptitude, learning styles, and sociocultural factors–affect language acquisition. We have beliefs about the effectiveness of explicit grammar instruction, the role of communicative activities, error correction, target language use, and strategies for teaching vocabulary. Our personal theories include beliefs about teaching tools and resources–the characteristics of a good textbook, the role of ancillary materials, and the incorporation of technology into our teaching. The development of our personal theories is a creative and dynamic process. They are formed through our personal and professional experiences and are continually refined and adapted throughout our lives (Richardson, 1996). A substantial body of literature supports the notion that teachers draw upon their personal pedagogical theories in establishing instructional goals, choosing methods, and performing other classroom behaviors.[1]

Research suggests that changes in pedagogical practices result from changes in teachers' personal theories (Glisan, 1996; Tedick & Walker, 1996; Richardson & Anders, 1994; Joiner, 1993). The failure to consider teachers' beliefs and attitudes has been attributed as one factor in the lack of success in earlier curricular change efforts (Darling-Hammond, 1990). Ellis (1986) maintains, "Teachers who operate in accordance with implicit beliefs may be not only uncritical but also resistant to change" (pp. 2-3). The design of the FLEQ encourages respondents to examine their implicit beliefs about language learning and teaching.

Class Participants

During spring 1999 and 2000, flyers announcing the course were mailed to 400 foreign language teachers in a large metropolitan area. Fourteen teachers (8 female, 6 male) enrolled in the 1999 class; 15 teachers (11 female, 4 male) enrolled in the 2000 class. Seven teachers in 1999 and 12 teachers in 2000 held bachelor's degree; the others held master's degrees. Their teaching experience ranged from 1 year to 26 years, with a median of 11 years' experience, in the 1999 class and from less than 1 year to 28 years, with a median of 5 years' experience, in the 2000 class. Spanish was the most commonly taught language among the participants in both classes; however, French and German were represented. The majority of teachers in both classes teach at the 9-12 level, but there was at least one middle school foreign language teacher and at least one elementary school foreign language teacher in both classes. In addition, in the 2000 class there was one university instructor.

Development of the FLEQ

On the basis of my study of the national standards document, other publications on the standards, and conference presentations on the standards, key ideas that represent fundamental assumptions underlying the standards have emerged, from which eight constructs were derived. For each of the eight constructs, I drafted between two and eight defining statements for a total of 41 statements. Respondents to the FLEQ indicate the extent of their agreement with the defining statements on a five-point Likert scale (strongly agree, agree, undecided, disagree, strongly disagree). Twenty-three of the defining statements (indicated by superscript ° in the following discussion) are worded so that agreement indicates consistency with the standards. The remaining 18 defining statements (indicated by * in the following discussion) are worded so that disagreement indicates consistency with the standards. As in other foreign language questionnaires, such as the FLAS (Garcia, Reynolds, & Savignon, 1976), the BALLI (Horwitz, 1985), the TBALLI (Horwitz, 1996), and the Bartz and Singer (1996) questionnaire, the FLEQ was not designed to yield a composite score. Rather, responses to each item of the FLEQ facilitate an identification and clarification of the respondents' beliefs and serve as a stimulus for discussion.

Each of the eight constructs upon which the FLEQ is based, along with the defining statements from the FLEQ corresponding to each construct, are discussed below.

A. Foreign language study is for all students, regardless of educational and career objectives, home language, and learning ability.

Historically, foreign language study has been somewhat elitist. Only the academically strong, college-bound students have pursued courses in foreign languages. Also, heritage students (those students whose home language is a language other than English) have not been encouraged to pursue courses in their home language. The philosophy underlying the standards is that all students– college bound and non-college bound, academically strong and academically challenged, students whose home language is English, and heritage students–should study a foreign language.

Eight statements in the FLEQ refer to construct A:

5° All students, regardless of career objectives, should study a foreign language.

14* Foreign language study is not for students who have difficulties with learning in general.

22° All students, regardless of future educational plans, should study a foreign language.

26* Students should not enroll in a language course if their home language is the language of the course.

28* The study of foreign languages will enhance only certain professions.

31° Students from non-English speaking backgrounds should enroll in courses in their home (native) language.

35* Only college-bound students should enroll in foreign language courses.

41° Students who have learning difficulties can be successful foreign language learners.

B. In order to reach the proficiency levels described in the standards, students should begin foreign language study in early elementary school.

Traditionally, sequential study of a foreign language has begun in high school. Although some junior high and middle schools may offer foreign languages, many students from these programs generally start over with level I in high school. And, even though foreign language programs at the elementary school (FLES) do exist in certain school districts, FLES is certainly not the national norm. The standards maintain that students should begin a sequential study of foreign language in early elementary school and continue to develop their skills throughout elementary, middle, and high school at progressively higher proficiency levels.

Two statements in the FLEQ refer to construct B:

6* Ideally, foreign language study should begin in high school.

36° Ideally, foreign language study should begin in early elementary school.

C. Language must be perceived as subject (that which acts) rather than as object (that which is acted upon).

Traditional foreign language instruction, based on a structuralist approach, assumes that language can be broken down into its smallest components to be examined and analyzed. Instruction is usually teacher-directed and often progresses in a page-by-page covering of the textbook, whereby students practice grammar and vocabulary by completing rote exercises. Then, if time permits, communicative activities are included. Such a curriculum is driven by the textbook, and the teacher's primary role is to cover x-number of chapters in the belief that students will be ready for the next level of instruction. Contrastingly, the role of grammar and discrete vocabulary in standards-based foreign language instruction is to support communication. A standards-based curriculum is guided by students' needs and interests, with the textbook and its ancillary materials serving as only two of many tools and resources.

Five statements in the FLEQ refer to construct C:

1*   Before students can communicate in the language, they must first learn the grammar.

7*   It is important to cover everything in the textbook.

15* The teacher's primary role is to help students learn what is in the textbook.

32° Students should use materials intended for same-age speakers of the target language.

38° Foreign language instruction should incorporate extensive use of authentic materials.

D. Culture and language are inextricably connected, and, therefore, culture must be an integrated aspect of language learning.

Typically, cultural instruction has played a rather passive role in foreign language classrooms. It has served primarily as an add-on to make the class more interesting or to provide relief from grammar instruction. It has been defined dichotomously as "Big C" and "little c." More often than not, specific cultural objectives have not been identified, and testing has consisted of little more than asking students to restate the facts from the textbook's short cultural section. The standards view "Big C" and "little c" as inseparable and define culture as consisting of three interrelated components: products, practices, and perspectives. In standards-based foreign language instruction, culture is an integral part of language instruction. Thus, specific cultural student learning objectives are defined and assessed just as systematically as grammatical and lexical objectives. Culture instruction consists of strategies that lead students to an understanding of the perspectives behind the products and practices, allowing them to engage in sensitive and meaningful interaction with people form the target culture(s).

Six statements in the FLEQ refer to construct D:

2*   The division of culture into "Big C" (literature, art, music, architecture), and "little c" (aspects of daily living) is a practical strategy for teaching culture in today's foreign language classes.

9*   Strategies for teaching culture should focus on facts about the culture(s) in which the target language is spoken.

18*   Culture is important, but vocabulary and grammar should be covered first.

25°   Only those who understand the culture(s) in which the language is spoken can be proficient in the language.

30°   Units of study should be organized around cultural themes.

34°   Culture instruction should include strategies that enable students to understand the underlying values of the target society.

E. The content of foreign language classes should go beyond that of vocabulary, grammar, and culture. Interdisciplinary content, as well as topics drawn from students' interests and background knowledge should be included.

Traditionally, the content of foreign language instruction, as defined by the textbook, has focused primarily on the language system: pronunciation, spelling, vocabulary, grammar, and syntax. Knowledge of the language system in standards-based foreign language instruction is perceived as providing a means for communicating, gaining cultural understanding, and connecting with other disciplines. The standards maintain that students use their emerging language skills to discuss interesting content, including content from other classes and topics in which students have an interest and prior knowledge.

Six statements in the FLEQ refer to construct E:

11°   The foreign language teacher should provide opportunities for students to make connections between the content of the foreign language class and the content of other classes students are taking.

12*   Most of the class time should be devoted to learning the language system (i.e., pronunciation, vocabulary, grammar, spelling, and syntax.)

19*   Foreign language instruction should focus primarily on the memorization of vocabulary and grammar rules.

23°   Grammar instruction is useful only to the extent that it enables students to make use of the language for communication.

24* Classroom instruction should focus primarily on building students' listening, speaking, reading, and writing skills.

29° The foreign language teacher should create opportunities for learning that connect what students already know with foreign language instruction.

F. Foreign language students should explore, develop, and use communication skills, learning strategies, critical thinking skills, and technology skills.

Traditionally, foreign language instruction has followed a four-skills approach: listening, reading, speaking, and writing. The standards are based on a broader perspective of foreign language study, which recognizes that the four-skills paradigm does not entirely reflect how learners learn or how people communicate. The standards perceive the content of foreign language instruction as a weave of curricular elements in which the standards' five goal areas (communication, cultures, connections, comparisons, and communities) are intertwined with seven content areas (the language system, cultural knowledge, communication strategies, critical thinking skills, learning strategies, other subject areas, and technology).

Six statements in the FLEQ refer to construct F:

3* The four skills approach (i.e., listening, reading, writing, speaking) to foreign language instruction is appropriate for today's foreign language programs.

4° Some instructional time should be devoted to teaching students how to use specific communication strategies (e.g., circumlocution, interpreting gestures, making predictions).

10° Foreign language instruction should include opportunities for students to develop and use technology skills.

17° Foreign language teachers should plan instruction on how to make use of specific learning strategies (e.g., use of formal rules, deliberate rehearsal, contextual guessing, seeking opportunities for comprehensible input).

21° Foreign language teachers should employ a variety of instructional materials.

33° Instruction in the foreign language class should be designed to promote the use of critical thinking skills.

G. Foreign language students should have opportunities to use the language beyond the classroom.

Traditionally, foreign language instruction has attempted to prepare students for the day when they might have an opportunity to travel to a country in which the target language is spoken. The standards maintain that students should use the language as they are developing proficiency, both in the school outside the foreign language classroom and beyond (e.g., locally in the community and abroad through letters, e-mail, audiotapes, and videotapes).

Two statements in the FLEQ refer to construct G:

8° Foreign language students should have opportunities to use the foreign language in the community.
38° Foreign language students should have in-school opportunities, outside the foreign language class, to share their knowledge of the target language and culture with other students in the school.

H. Assessment should be authentic and performance-based and measured through portfolios, projects, oral proficiency testing, and other open-ended activities.

Traditionally, foreign language assessment has been carried out using end-of-the-chapter discrete point tests of grammar and vocabulary that stressed recognition and breadth of knowledge. Even though standards-based foreign language instruction incorporates testing of grammar and vocabulary for formative evaluation, the role of assessment is perceived to directly measure performance, what students can actually do in the language. Performance in the language requires depth of learning.

Six statements in the FLEQ refer to construct H:

13* Assessment should focus primarily on students' knowledge of specific grammar points.
16° Assessment should include consideration of the students' thinking processes.
20* Chapter tests generally provide an adequate means of assessment.
27° Assessment should directly measure the students' ability to perform in the language.
39° Open-ended activities (e.g., portfolios, demonstrations, presentations, projects) should be the primary means by which students are assessed.
40* Students should be tested on everything that is in the chapter.

Responses to the FLEQ

The responses to the pre- and post-administrations of the FLEQ for the 1999 and 2000 classes were submitted to separate paired sample t-tests.[2] The means of the participants' responses on the Likert scale of 1 to 5, as determined by the data analysis, can be classified into three categories:

A) Responses consistent with the standards: means between 1 and 2.6 for the 23 statements worded so that agreement indicates consistency with the standards (identified by ° in preceding discussion), and means between 5 and 4.4 for the 18 statements worded so that disagreement indicates consistency with the standards (identified by * in the preceding discussion).

B) Responses that indicate participants were undecided: means ranging from 2.7 through 4.3.

C) Responses inconsistent with the standards: means between 5 and 4.4 for the 23 statements worded so that agreement indicates consistency with the standards (indicated by ° in the preceding discussion), and means between 1 and 2.6 for the 18 statements worded so that disagreement indicates consistency with the standards (identified by * in the preceding discussion).

Table 1, on the next page, provides the total number and the percentage of statements for each of the three categories for the pre and post FLEQ in both the 1999 and the 2000 class.

Table 1

Total number & percentage of responses to statements in three categories			
	Consistent with Standards	Undecided	Inconsistent with Standards
1999 class			
Pre-FLEQ	19 (46%)	19 (46%)	3 (7%)
Post-FLEQ	34 (83%)	7 (17%)	0
2000 class			
Pre-FLEQ	25 (61%)	12 (29%)	4 (10%)
Post-FLEQ	35 (85%)	6 (15%)	0

The paired sample t-tests indicated that the difference between the pre-FLEQ and the post-FLEQ means was significant for 12 statements (29%) in the 1999 class (statements 31, 32, 2, 9, 18, 25, 11, 24, 3, 10, 8, and 39) and 13 statements (32%) in the 2000 class (statements 2, 9, 18, 30, 34, 12, 24, 3, 10, 13, 27, 39, and 40). Of the statements for which there was a significant difference in means, 7 statements (17%) (statements 2, 9, 18, 24, 3, 10, and 39) were common to both classes.

Discussion

Data presented in Table 1 seem to indicate that during the time in which the teachers participated in the professional development course, they were engaged in the process of identifying and clarifying their pedagogical beliefs. The FLEQ appears to be a heuristic instrument for stimulating the process and illustrating the shifts in perspective as teachers examine their existing beliefs about foreign language teaching and learning.

The analysis of the responses to the FLEQ provides insight into the professional development needs of foreign language teachers as they work toward implementing the standards. The statements about which teachers in both classes changed their beliefs to a significant degree concerned culture, the four skills approach, technology, and assessment. This finding may be an indication that professional development in these areas is especially needed.

Because of the reciprocal nature of teachers' beliefs and practices, it cannot be assumed that identifying one's pedagogical beliefs by responding to the FLEQ during a professional development course is enough to effect change in the classroom. Follow-up research involving the classroom practices of teachers who participate in the course and respond to the FLEQ should be conducted. The research would investigate the instructional goals, methods, and other classroom behaviors of the teachers. Are their classroom practices consistent with their beliefs as revealed by the FLEQ? If not, are there circumstances in the school environment that exert a stronger influence upon teachers' classroom practices than their own pedagogical beliefs? What impediments exist that prevent teachers from teaching in a way that is consistent with their beliefs? What can be done to eliminate or alleviate those impediments? Research which addresses the preceding questions, along with continued use of the FLEQ in professional development, will lead teachers to a greater understanding of their pedagogical beliefs and teacher educators to a greater understanding of the needs of foreign language teachers as they work toward implementing standards-based foreign language instruction.

Notes

[1]   For comprehensive reviews of literature on the relationship between teachers' beliefs and actions, see Richardson (1996), Kagan (1992), and Clark and Peterson (1986).

[2]   The risk of the occurrence of a Type I error is increased when multiple t-tests are performed. According to Gall, Borg, and Gall (1996, pp. 39-391), the risk of Type I error can be reduced by setting the probability level low (e.g., p=.01).

References

Anderson, R. D. (1995). Curriculum reform: Dilemmas and promise. *Phi Delta Kappan, 77* (1), 33-36.

Bailey, K. M., Bergthold, B., Braunstein, N. J., Holbrook, M. P., Tuman, J., Waissbluth, X., & Zambo, L. J. (1996). The language learner's autobiography: Examining the "apprenticeship of observation." In D. Freeman & J. C. Richards (Eds.), *Teacher learning in language teaching* (pp. 11-19). Cambridge: Cambridge University Press.

Bartz, W. H., & Singer, M. K. (1996). The programmatic implications of foreign language standards. In R.C. Lafayette (Ed.), *National standards: A catalyst for reform* (pp. 139-167). Lincolnwood, IL: National Textbook Company.

Clark, C. M., & Peterson, P. L. (1986). Teachers' thought processes. In M. C. Wittrock (Ed.), *Handbook of research on teaching* (3rd ed.) (pp.255-296). New York: Macmillan.

Darling-Hammond, L. (1990). Instructional policy into practice: "The power of the bottom over the top." *Educational Evaluation and Policy Analysis, 12* (3), 339-347.

Ellis, R. (1986). *Understanding second language acquisition.* Oxford: Oxford University Press.

Gall, M. D., Borg, W. R., & Gall, J. P. (1996). *Educational research: An introduction* (6th ed.). New York: Longman.

Garcia, R. de., Reynolds, S., & Savignon, S. (1976). Foreign-language attitude survey. *The Canadian Modern Language Review, 32,* 302-304.

Glisan, E. W. (1996). A collaborative approach to professional development. In R. C. Lafayette (Ed.), *National standards: A catalyst for reform* (pp. 57-96). Lincolnwood, IL: National Textbook Company.

Horwitz, E. K. (1985). Using student beliefs about language learning and teaching in the foreign language methods course. *Foreign Language Annals, 18,* 333-340.

Horwitz, E. K. (1996). Meeting the cognitive and emotional needs of new foreign language teachers. In Z. Moore (Ed.), *Foreign language teacher education* (pp. 289-299). Lanham, MD: University Press of America.

Joiner, G. (1993). Reflecting on teacher development. In G. Guntermann (Ed.), *Developing language teachers for a changing world* (pp. 187-212). Lincolnwood, IL: National Textbook Company.

Kagan, D. M. (1992). Professional growth among preservice and beginning teachers. *Review of Educational Research, 62* (2), 129-169.

Leighton, M. S., & Sykes, G. (1992). *The professionalization of teaching: A centerpiece of Kentucky reform.* Charleston, WV: State Policy Program, Appalachia Educational Laboratory.

Little, J. W. (1993). Teachers' professional development in a climate of educational reform. *Educational Evaluation and Policy Analysis, 15* (2), 129-151.

National Standards in Foreign Language Education Project. (1996). *Standards for foreign language learning: Preparing for the 21st century.* Lawrence, KS: Allen Press.

National Standards in Foreign Language Education Project. (1999). *Standards for foreign language learning in the 21st century.* Lawrence, KS: Allen Press.

Richardson, V. (1996). The role of attitudes and beliefs in learning to teach. In J. Sikula (Ed.), *Handbook of research on teacher education* (2nd ed.) (pp. 102-119). New York: Association of Teacher Educators.

Richardson, V., & Anders, P. L. (1994). The study of teacher change. In V. Richardson (Ed.), *Teacher change and the staff development process* (pp. 159-180). New York: Teachers College Press.

Sparks, D. (1994). Staff development implications of national board certification: An interview with NBPTS's James Smith. *Journal of Staff Development, 15* (1), 58-59.

Tedick, J., & Walker, C. L. (1996). R(T)eaching all students: Necessary changes in teacher education. In B. H. Wing (Ed.), *Foreign languages for all: Challenges and choices* (pp. 187-220). Report of the Northeast Conference on the Teaching of Foreign Languages. Lincolnwood, IL: National Textbook Company.

Wagner, E. D. (1993). *New directions for American education: Implications for continuing educators.* Washington, D.C.: Office of Educational Research and Improvement.

5

Development and Dissemination of the *Indiana Academic Standards for Foreign Languages:* Teacher Teamwork at the Forefront of the Project

Kristin Hoyt-Oukada
Indiana Department of Education

Introduction: From the Proficiency Movement to Standards

In the recent past, the foreign language profession has witnessed curricular and instructional innovation of a paradigmatic nature in response to the proficiency movement, officially ushered in with the 1986 publication of the *ACTFL Proficiency Guidelines.* These guidelines in particular have generated intense dialectics and prompted the creation of numerous curricular and instructional models, such as the focus on communicative tasks as an organizing principle for planning, structuring, and prioritizing language instruction. The traditional grammar-driven approach to language planning was called into question–its validity challenged. The proficiency movement and dialogues that ensued brought about serious and dramatic developments in foreign language education: (1) a growing practice of involving students in expressing themselves in the target language; (2) an increased ability to assess oral skills; (3) sensibility to students' learning styles and preferences; (4) attentiveness to authenticity and believability of language use; (5) valorization of personalized classroom activities; (6) consideration of pertinence and age-appropriateness; (7) preference for contextualized language instruction; and (8) replacement of the teacher-centered classroom based on a transmission model with collaborative partner work or student-to-student interaction.

As with the advent of any educational paradigm, there are those who have fully embraced the proficiency movement just as there are some who are reluctant to endorse it, and surely many who fall somewhere in between. There are certainly few situations and few individuals, however, that remain entirely untouched by the message of proficiency. As a profession nationwide, we have made considerable progress in improving the quality of foreign language instruction and we are still exploring better ways to organize teaching objectives around proficiency, to design instruction with a focus on communication, and to assess the various levels of a learner's ascension toward full proficiency. And today, our progress has reached the next logical concern: accountability and standards, a concern we share with our colleagues in all fields of education. Across the subject-area disciplines and across the preK-16 levels of instruction, including students, teachers, programs, and institutions, the eyes of educators, community members, and politicians alike are focusing on accountability and standards across the nation. Foreign language has not been exempt from this national sweep. In fact, advocacy efforts and collaboration within the profession secured a place for foreign language in the national movement with the Goals 2000 initiative and the drafting of national standards in seven core subject areas.[1] The standards movement has ushered in a heightened focus on the learner, with attention to specific expectancies and measurable outcomes of students' proficiencies at various stages and levels of learning.

Conceptualization of the *Indiana Academic Standards for Foreign Languages (IASFL):* The Tradition of Curriculum Planning in Indiana and the National Standards as a New Framework

Indiana has been in a vanguard position as the profession has grown and evolved from the proficiency movement to accountability and standards. As ACTFL was publishing the *Proficiency Guidelines*, Indiana was publishing *A Guide to Proficiency-Based Instruction in Modern Languages for Indiana Schools* (1986), a particularly timely document that introduced the notion of communicative competencies to Indiana educators. The next major curricular publication to be developed by the Indiana Department of Education was the *Indiana Foreign Language Proficiency Guide* (1995). This document centered on (1) goals, defining the major purposes of foreign language education; (2) content standards, defining what students should know and be able to do to address the goals; and (3) sample performances, examples of how students might meet particular content standards. The strong connection of the *Indiana Foreign Language Proficiency Guide* to the national standards, being drafted at the same time, was evidenced in the notion of content standards. And just a few years later, in response to the *Standards for Foreign Language Learning: Preparing for the 21ˢᵗ Century,* published in 1996, Indiana engaged in the process of drafting a new state document, even more closely aligned to the national standards.

As the established history and tradition in Indiana, state-supported foreign language curriculum projects have included local teachers as key participants. Classroom teachers have been included as active contributors and co-creators in articulating and assessing the development of curriculum documents and materials. The state's leadership in bringing together people and resources has been and continues to be an effective design for professional development, creating working arenas where teachers network in learning together and subsequently carry their skills and understandings to the field for duplication of the collaborative working/learning process.

Development of the *IASFL*: Teacher Engagement in the Drafting Act and Balancing Act

The state standards curriculum work was initiated in the autumn of 1998 with a public call-out for participation in the Indiana standards writing team. The importance and meaningfulness of creating a state standards document for foreign languages drew a positive response, and selection of the writing task force was in place by the end of the year. The following year, a nine-month decision-making period ensued during which the compelling task of structuring the new Indiana foreign language standards document was undertaken. Proposals for the content, structure, and format of the new Indiana document included consideration of the national and other states' standards documents, among other suggestions. The group consensus was to create a customized curriculum framework that would be both consistent with the national standards framework and responsive to the context in which foreign language education operates in the State of Indiana. That is, the teacher task force was committed to converting the ideologies of the national standards into a teachers' document pointing toward practical classroom application; to mediating the theoretical and abstract ideas being discussed and proposed on the national scene in the standards movement and the practical needs and wants of classroom practitioners in a usable document. Teamwork skills of negotiation, communication, and accommodation were at work as task force members joined in working toward a shared vision of purpose.

The task force initially agreed upon a framework based upon the national standards, (the five Cs of *communication*, *cultures*, *connections*, *comparisons*, and *communities*) and a format including three components:

(1) progress indicators; (2) classroom examples; and (3) scenarios. The framework and format were modified for three stages of learning (*beginning*, *developing*, and *expanding*). The concept of stages of learning was adopted because of its affinity to the idiosyncrasies of individual learners and the overlapping of competency levels within a single classroom, experienced by teachers on a daily basis. The ensuing task of drafting language to illustrate performance indicators of student progress, examples of classroom activities, and instructional scenarios was enthusiastically undertaken and carried out by the task force.[2] The creative task of drafting standards' language matched the shared interest of the writing task force, while at the same time afforded extensive opportunities for individualized participation of task force members. The eager participation of the task force was in keeping with one of the positive generalized perceptions of teachers as thriving in environments where creativity can flourish. Moreover, this particular teacher task force was called to exercise the patience and flexibility that teachers are also generally renowned for. As the months evolved and the planning, composing, and editing process unraveled, the reality of political decision-making and policies entered into the arena. Unlike previous curricular movements and eras of reform, the standards movement incorporates a broader spectrum of parties (e.g., parents, teachers, administrators, community members, policy makers, business and industry, etc.), each with vested interests in the process.

As the foreign language standards task force was bringing its work to closure in July of 1999, the Indiana General Assembly passed new legislation to strengthen academic standards. Under this legislation, it was determined that standards for Grades K-12 would be delineated in English/ language arts, mathematics, science, and social studies. Further, the Department of Education was granted authority to identify other subject areas for which standards could be developed. The Superintendent of Public Instruction, Dr. Suellen Reed, determined that the Office of Program Development, in the Center for School Improvement of the Department of Education, would be assigned the task of drafting K-12 standards for all academic subject areas, including foreign language. It was thus the wish and the directive of the Superintendent that all subject areas would create documents that outline state standards for each and all levels of instruction, including examples of student knowledge, skill, or performance as needed for illustrative purposes. In the interest of school administrators and the many teachers (particularly at the elementary level), as well as the community-at-large, it was determined that all subject area documents would follow the same design and format.

This decision created a new and different type of challenge for the Indiana foreign language standards task force, already seven months into the project of working with the foreign language consultant from the Office of Program Development of the State Department of Education in drafting the state standards document. Since the teaching of foreign languages in Indiana neither represents a subject area offered at all levels of instruction nor is a part of the core curriculum required for high school graduation, the possibility of creating a level-by-level K-12 document was a moot point. Though there are some isolated cases of foreign language offerings in Indiana elementary schools and yet more cases at the middle school level, there are presently only state-developed course descriptions for six levels of instruction, which are largely offered in high school settings. Consequently, the task force had to sacrifice their cherished notion of 'stages of learning' (beginning, developing, expanding) to accommodate the six levels of instruction (based on instructional sequence of courses and actual 'seat time') represented in foreign language education in the State of Indiana. Additionally, the task force was perplexed as to how to integrate its near-complete composition of progress indicators, classroom examples, and learning scenarios into the state-mandated format calling for simply standards statements and illustrative examples for the standards, as needed.

At this juncture, to reconcile the disparities at hand without forfeiting their work to date, the task force decided to continue their work and carry it forth to a point of closure with two documents: one, the *IASFL,* to satisfy the official requirements of the Department of Education and another, *A Guide for Implementing Indiana Academic Standards for Foreign Languages (IASFL),* a teacher resource companion document to fulfill their commitment to satisfying the needs and expectations of the classroom practitioner. Hence, the next months were spent bringing this dual task to completion. And, following a field review of the two draft documents, final editing, and approval by the State Board of Education, the *IASFL* and *A Guide for Implementing IASFL* were published in Summer 2000. This response of the task force to the apparent duality of (1) state centralized control and (2) practitioner-motivated planning was one of synthesis. While the push for needed reform through state mandates might chill teachers' receptivity to the standards, the abandonment of institutionalized approaches by bottom-up teacher networks might likewise be discredited by policymakers and have modest or spotted impact (Lieberman & Miller, 2000).

Dissemination of the *IASFL*: Teachers Training Teachers – Sharing the Process and the Product

The dissemination of the *IASFL* and the companion implementation guide was carried out by a another cadre of Indiana foreign language classroom teachers, drawn from the writing task force pool, following a planning and training workshop. Regional day-long in-service meetings were scheduled throughout the state, during which members of the newly organized cadre of teachers collaborated in presenting for the entire teaching community an overview of the two documents *(IASFL* and *A Guide for Implementing IASFL)*. The cadre also led teachers in familiarization activities related to the standards, use of the *Guide for Implementing IASFL* as a curriculum planning tool, along with orientation to and practice with reviewing and selecting textbooks based on the standards. Approximately thirty percent of the state's foreign language teachers attended dissemination workshops and overall the workshops were well-received. They provided a forum for community and collaboration, extending relationships beyond the traditional school or district level boundaries, as well as inviting teachers into the bigger picture beyond their personal classroom issues. The success of the standards dissemination workshops can be attributed to the pertinence and responsiveness of their design as well as to their philosophy of teamwork, summed up in the aphorism, "for teachers, by teachers."

The philosophy behind the teamwork model used in Indiana foreign language curriculum development and dissemination for nearly two decades is based on two convictions: (1) professional growth is best developed through a multi-layered approach combining knowledge from the outside with knowledge from the inside; and (2) the mass of teachers in the field are more receptive to change when the innovation is presented in the format of horizontal and vertical collegial sharing; and conversely, they are reluctant to embrace innovation when change is prescribed on the basis of a top-down authoritative message. These two principles are reflected in evolving educational practice in addressing school reform, particularly staff development. The linear approach of disseminating empirical, outside findings from the top-down is increasingly being replaced by a multidirectional collaborative approach that allows teachers to cooperate in discovering arenas for professional growth, often under the guidance of a facilitator or coach who brings a necessary outside perspective while respecting the inside perspective and context of the teachers.

The initial training of the trainers, which occurred with the standards writing task force and the standards dissemination cadre, provided an opportunity for a small group of teachers to benefit and learn from the outside knowledge presented in the national standards and other states' standards documents, while incorporating their inside knowledge and experience from the classroom in forging new understandings. Training the trainers involved flexibility and risk-taking as teachers engaged in discussions of challenging issues that did not easily pose solutions and grappled with the task of transferring new ideas into written word. Training the trainers also required time and patience, as teachers struggled to clarify their understandings in comprehensible terms and explored strategies for transferring theoretical or conceptual knowledge into practical and realistic applications. Eventually the thinking and work of the teachers took over as their familiarity with outside knowledge and their confidence to rely on their own forged understandings sustained the group's efforts.

In like manner, the cadre members experienced another level of learning as they were compelled to exercise flexibility and patience as teacher-presenters (during dissemination workshops) sharing outside and newly acquired knowledge with their colleagues in the field. Each level of transmission incorporated support for teachers to extend their vast personal understandings already in place with new ideas and approaches.[3] The teacher-directed workshops provided an arena for   teachers to be empowered for effective curriculum planning, as curriculum designers, not merely consumers of an outside curriculum. Beyond orientation to the standards, the principle message of the disseminations workshops was a call to customize curriculum planning based on local contexts and needs, using the *IASFL* (and by extension, the national standards) as a framework. This message was in harmony with the notion of respect for outside knowledge and inside knowledge. Workshops generally provide a forum for transmission of information (outside knowledge) as well as incorporate some level of hands-on participation (inside knowledge). However, it must be acknowledged that the workshop format holds inherent limitations as well. With innovative approaches such as the standards movement, the depth of understanding necessary for adoption and change cannot be accomplished in workshops alone.

Conclusion: Teachers as Classroom Pioneers Implementing the *IASFL*

It might be fair conjecture to suggest that the standards writing task force and dissemination cadre members are a majority among those Indiana classroom practitioners currently engaged in planning, developing, or implementing a standards-based curriculum in their schools. The extended opportunities from which these teachers benefited is measured not only in mere hours of standards-related work, but more importantly in collaborative engagement with colleagues on standards-related issues. Where the (orientation) workshops left off, the classroom teacher is called to pick up the charge. However, to the degree that important change needs to take place, the classroom teacher must engage beyond the surface level to enact real and significant change.

One of the emerging notions in educational reform, as schools and school personnel nationwide struggle to measure up to the increasing calls and demands for accountability, is the understanding that contexts are critical to change (Lieberman & Miller, 2000). Meaningful change occurs at the locus of action and reflection on personal practice. The task force and cadre members benefited from such a context where ample time and a collegial environment fostered reflection. However, teachers today are increasingly swallowed up by the demands of preparation, instruction, and grading, combined with the necessary contacts outside of class time including both students and parents, not to mention building level responsibilities, and the list goes on. Although clearly a tremendous challenge, teachers are compelled nonetheless to carve out some time to address their own professional development in the absence of organizational provisions for such. The nation's eyes increasingly consider teachers as accountable for their own professionalism and the consequent student performance. And, one of the important claims of the 1986 report, *A Nation Prepared,* is that teachers engaged as leaders in curriculum, instruction, and assessment hold the keys to student success. Moreover, teachers are included in the mandate to model, in their own growth and development, the current constructivist understandings of cognition and learning, maintaining that learners must be active co-creators of their learning experiences.

As teachers embark upon carrying the standards message beyond the initial level of having the documents in-hand and possessing a basic familiarization with their contents, the sagacity of embarking upon a journey in collaboration with other pioneers is not to be minimized. Formal or informal interaction between two or more educators with a shared vision promises fruitful and meaningful growth. There are many collaborative venues of opportunity for exploring the standards, where teachers can support one another, e.g., action research, case study, journaling, mentoring, coaching, study groups, etc. And, there continues to be a growing repertoire of print and electronic resources in support of standards-based curriculum planning, instruction, and assessment.

Indiana finds itself on the cusp of an exciting era in foreign language education as increasingly more teachers are oriented to the *IASFL* and more foreign language departments engage in standards-based curriculum planning. There are scattered pockets of teacher groups highly engaged in the process; among them an action research team that is purposefully pursuing implementation of a standards-approach in their planning, instruction, and assessment. This group is generating models based on their classroom research, with the intent of sharing these models for statewide use in guiding others in the standards quest.

The invitation to get on the standards train, in Indiana as elsewhere in the US, is not for a short excursion. Unlike never before in US educational reform movements, the standards movement crosses traditional boundaries and domains, incorporating all levels and arenas of education. The call to accountability has left no one out. There currently exists a plethora of standards (e.g., student standards for PreK-16, teacher standards for all levels and subjects of instruction, organizational standards for schools and universities, standards for staff development, etc.), and the next few years certainly will witness the broadening of this scope. Those having a vested interest in school reform also include a broader audience than has traditionally been incorporated into this realm. To join the standards movement is not only a step toward full participation in the teaching profession, it is a personal investment in professional growth and development.

Notes

[1] In response to information regarding the U.S. Department of Education's intention to fund the development of standards, ACTFL, AATF, AATG and AATSP collaborated in determining standards for foreign languages. By January 1993, foreign language was granted status as the seventh and final core curriculum subject area and subsequently received funding for the development of K-12 standards.

[2] A year prior to undertaking the drafting of the *IASFL*, the State participated in supporting a group of Indiana foreign language educators who
initiated the drafting of learning scenarios for learners of various languages. These learning scenarios were incorporated into the work of the
standards writing team, and eventually many of the scenarios were included in the *Guide for Implementing IASFL*. The learning scenario writing
team also operated on the "for teachers, by teachers" model. The teachers
worked in small groups, learning from one another as they embraced the
standards framework. The teachers collaborated in the process of drafting, critiquing, and revising as the writing of the learning scenarios
evolved.

[3] The top-down/bottom-up (outside knowledge/inside knowledge) synthe-
sized model aptly addresses the concerns of teachers who presently face
seemingly overwhelming calls for change. The emotional charge of such
concerns was witnessed in the ambiguity of the messages: "How *dare*
you tell me what to do!" "Just *tell me* what to do!" which surfaced at
different times and in various ways throughout the dissemination process.

References

American Council on the Teaching of Foreign Languages. (1986). *ACTFL
Proficiency Guidelines*. Hastings-on-Hudson, NY: American Council
on the Teaching of Foreign Languages.

Indiana Department of Education. (2000). *Indiana academic standards for
foreign languages*. Indianapolis, IN: I-DOE Publications.

Indiana Department of Education. (2000). *A guide for implementing* Indiana academic standards for foreign languages. Indianapolis, IN: I-DOE
Publications.

Lieberman, A., & Miller, L. (2000). Teaching and teacher development: A
new synthesis for a new century. In R. S. Brandt (Ed.), *Education in a
new era: ASDC yearbook 2000*. Alexandria, VA: Association for Supervision and Curriculum Development.

National Standards in Foreign Language Education Project. (1996). *Standards for foreign language learning: Preparing for the 21st century*.
Lawrence, KS: Allen Press.

Carnegie Corporation of New York. (1986). *A nation prepared: Teachers
for the 21st century*. New York: Carnegie Corporation of New York.

6

Writing Activities and Assessments for Today's Classrooms: A Step-by-Step Approach

Donna Reseigh Long and Janice L. Macián
The Ohio State University

Introduction

In the early 1980s, writing instruction in both first (L1) and second language (L2) began to focus more on the experience (process) of writing and less on the outcome (product). Since that time, researchers have published extensively on this topic (see, for example: Flower and Hayes, 1981; Gaudiani, 1981; Krashen, 1984). The consensus of these writing experts is that writing (like other aspects of language) develops in stages over time. Studies of skilled vs. unskilled writers have shown that skilled writers tend to focus on planning, revising, and sending a clear message. Unskilled writers, on the other hand, tend to focus on mechanics and spend little time in planning and revising (see, for example: Magnan, 1985; Richards, 1990). In addition to the theoretical dialogue, pedagogical guides to writing now abound in print (see, for example: Shrum and Glisan, 1994; Scott, 1996) and online (see, for example: Ohio ESL. The Writing Process, August 15, 2000. Available: http://www.ohiou.edu/esl/english/writing/process.html; Purdue University Online Writing Lab. October 4, 2000. Available: http://owl.english.purdue.edu). In reviewing the literature, we find that researchers and teachers agree: it takes time and practice to develop good writing skills.

In our collective experience as language teachers and teacher educators, we have found teaching and assessing writing skills to be among our most challenging tasks. Over the years, we incorporated process approaches, prose models, peer editing, and a variety of assessment techniques into our beginning and intermediate Spanish programs at The Ohio State University. Through extensive experimentation, we developed an eclectic step-by-step approach that works in our large language program with classes that are taught primarily by inexperienced graduate teaching associates and part-time lecturers. Our approach consists of four broad phases: planning, writing, revising, and assessing. This approach helps students focus on the process of writing by requiring them to plan, write, revise, and assess their own work. The remainder of this article describes our approach and presents an extended model that may be adapted to different languages and various levels of instruction.

The secret to our success is the size and order of the steps within each phase. In our approach, we start with idea generation and continue through the writing process by well-defined steps until the final assessment is made. The example presented in this article is narration, a topic that may be easily adapted to other kinds of writing tasks for beginning, intermediate, or advanced writers. In our Spanish language program, we teach description, narration, and various types of explication (comparison/contrast, analysis, persuasion, etc.) at the beginning, intermediate, and advanced levels, incorporating appropriate vocabulary, structures, and themes at each level. In this example, we focus on first-year Spanish students who have studied the past tense (preterit and imperfect). Although Spanish is the language of instruction in our classes, for the sake of clarity in this article, we present the steps in English, with examples in Spanish.

Teaching Narration Step by Step

Phase I: Planning
Step 1: Explain what you mean
Tell students what you mean by narration. Although they have probably read some type of narration in the past, they may not understand the technical term. A simple definition with examples will suffice, such as:

> Narration is the act or process of telling a story or giving
> an account of a happening. Some common types of narra-
> tion include newspaper articles, short stories, legends,
> histories, biographies, and novels.

Step 2: Activate background knowledge
Virtually all students who are enrolled in language courses have read some form of narration...a newspaper article, a legend, a short story, or a novel. Begin by having students recall what they know about narration. Use a familiar example, such as a story that is part of the students' language arts curriculum or a well-known fairy tale. Encourage them by asking simple questions:

- What is the setting?
- What is the time frame for the actions?
- Who does the narrating?
- Who are the characters?
- Are the events real or fictitious?

Step 3: Review old concepts

At this point, it is worthwhile to have a quick review of the verb tenses that students will use when writing a narration. In Spanish, for example, the past tense has two aspects, imperfect and preterit, each with its own specific uses. Beginning language learners can also narrate in the present, a familiar technique used in telling anecdotes and jokes in casual conversation.

Step 4: Teach new concepts

We like to teach the concepts of narrator (limited and omniscient) and point of view (first person, third person) before proceeding. Again, the explanation can be simplified. An omniscient narrator is familiar with both the actions and the thoughts of the characters. A limited narrator can only report their actions. A first-person narrator tells the story from his/her own perspective, using the "I" verb forms. A third-person narrator tells the story from the perspective of an outsider, using the "he/she" verb forms. Provide examples to reinforce the concepts:

Primera persona:

"'Hija, no estás gordita, sino llena de vida.' Seguramente, estas palabras les son familiares a muchas latinas como yo, pues, hasta donde recuerdo, son las palabras que oía decir a mi madre cuando la familia y los amigos me hacían bromas por estar un poquito gorda (Landeros, 2000)".

> *"'Daughter, you aren't fat, but full of life.' Surely, these words are familiar to many Latinas like myself, well, as far back as I remember, these are the words that I heard my mother say when my family and friends made fun of me for being a bit chubby...."*

Tercera persona:

"Juan Gutiérrez, joven gallardo, delgado, flaco, de piel blanca como leche porque nunca vio el sol, pasaba sus días y noches conectado a su ciberespacio...(Conde, 1999)".

"Juan Gutiérrez, a smart young man, thin, skin milk white because he never saw the sun, spent his days and nights connected to his cyberspace..."

For learners of Spanish, we also teach the concepts of background (**el trasfondo**) and foreground (**el primer plano**), because of their relationship to the two aspects of the past tense. Background information is narrated in the imperfect, while foreground actions are narrated in the preterit. Here are some examples:

Trasfondo: Afuera *llovía* y *hacía* mucho viento...
               It was raining and very windy outdoors...

Primer plano: ...mientras adentro *escuchamos* un grito de terror.
               ...while inside we heard a scream of terror.

We also like to emphasize the importance of good introductions and conclusions for any type of writing. Without a reminder, we find that many students tend to jump directly into the "action" without thinking about their readers and trying to catch their attention. In addition, they often repeat ideas in the conclusion that were presented earlier in the composition, instead of summarizing or providing personal comments.

Step 5: Provide an example

We like to provide learners with an example in Spanish. Of course, we don't expect students to write like professional writers, but we have found that having learners analyze a professionally written example helps them focus more clearly on the mechanics of writing. Beginning students can work with magazine articles and interviews or excerpts from literature that incorporate previously introduced themes and vocabulary. Intermediate and advanced learners can analyze more difficult literary selections. Along with the example, we also include a list of unfamiliar vocabulary and some questions to use as a guide to comprehension. Then, we have students analyze the narration and complete a chart. Finally, we discuss the analysis as a whole class.

Analysis of the Example

Narrator: ❑ limited ❑ omniscient
Point of view ❑ first person ❑ third person
List of characters _____ _____
_____ _____
Background verbs _____ _____
_____ _____
Foreground verbs _____ _____

Step 6: Teach helpful words and phrases

Teach students the vocabulary that is typical of narration in your language. In Spanish, time and sequence vocabulary is the logical accompaniment to the imperfect and preterit grammar concepts.

Imperfecto: expresiones de repetición
Imperfect: expressions of repetition

a menudo–*frequently*	siempre–*always*
a veces–*sometimes*	todas las noches–*every evening*
de vez en cuando–*from time to time*	todas las tardes–*every afternoon*
generalmente–*generally*	todos los días–*every day*
los lunes, etc.–*on Mondays, etc.*	todos los meses–*every month*
normalmente–*normally*	todos los años–*every year*
	usualmente–*usually*

Pretérito: expresiones de tiempos definidos
Preterit: definite time expressions

a las cinco de la mañana–*at five a.m.*	el año pasado–*last year*
anoche–*last night*	el mes anterior–*the month before*
anteayer–*the day before yesterday*	el sábado pasado–*last Saturday*
ayer–*yesterday*	esta mañana–*this morning* ·

Step 7: Generate ideas

Working in pairs or small groups, learners brainstorm different topics suitable for a narration. State the general theme, which may be related to the current unit of study. In small groups, for example, students can discuss past celebrations in which they have participated, describing the guests, the activities, and the foods. These types of activities not only help students get ideas for their compositions, but they also help them focus on related structures and vocabulary.

Step 8: Specify the format

Provide students with format instructions (we find that written instructions are remembered better). If the composition is to be handwritten, have students write on every other line to make an easier task of editing. If the composition is to be typed, double spacing is a must. Specify other formatting issues, such as indenting the first line of each paragraph and using upper case for titles, bold face for headings, and italics for subheadings. College-level students can be asked to follow MLA or APA guidelines.

Step 9: Gather the nuts and bolts

Learners can now begin to work alone, although they are still in the planning stage. At this point they should specify the type of narrator and point of view that they wish to use in their narrations. They may wish to title their compositions before beginning to write, or they may wait until after they have written the first draft.

Phase 2: Writing

Step 10: Write the first draft

Students should now be ready to write the first draft. Emphasize that good writing takes practice; they will have to write more than one version of a writing task in order to achieve a satisfactory product.

Phase 3: Revising

Step 11: Revise the draft

After completing a draft that seems satisfactory to them, students should self-edit their compositions. Provide them with the following guidelines (adjusted to fit the characteristics of your language and your course objectives):

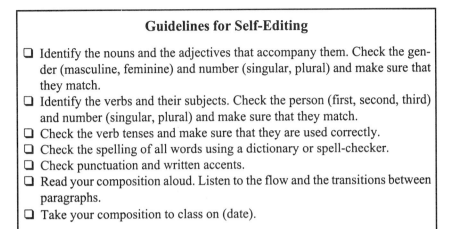

Guidelines for Self-Editing

❑ Identify the nouns and the adjectives that accompany them. Check the gender (masculine, feminine) and number (singular, plural) and make sure that they match.

❑ Identify the verbs and their subjects. Check the person (first, second, third) and number (singular, plural) and make sure that they match.

❑ Check the verb tenses and make sure that they are used correctly.

❑ Check the spelling of all words using a dictionary or spell-checker.

❑ Check punctuation and written accents.

❑ Read your composition aloud. Listen to the flow and the transitions between paragraphs.

❑ Take your composition to class on (date).

Step 12: Show the draft to someone else

Peer editing works best when students work in pairs and have specific guidelines to follow. The teacher should float from group to group, keeping students on task and making specific suggestions. This step is time-consuming, but beneficial. We use a Spanish version of the following guidelines in our classes. The simple yes/no format is easy for students to use, yet provides the writer with feedback on both content and structure.

Guidelines for Peer-Editing

Content

yes no   The introduction gets the reader's attention.
yes no   The organization is logical.
yes no   The composition presents interesting ideas.
yes no   The transitions between paragraphs are smooth.
yes no   The conclusion does not repeat the introduction.

Vocabulary

yes no   The vocabulary can be visualized.
yes no   The adjectives are descriptive.
yes no   The verbs are concrete and active (avoid overuse of *to be* & *there are*).
yes no   *Ser* and *estar* are used correctly.

Correctness

yes no   Subject/verb agreement is correct.
yes no   Verb tenses are correct.
yes no   Noun/adjective agreement is correct.
yes no   Spelling of all words is correct.
yes no   Punctuation of all sentences is correct.

You may also ask students to give each other a preliminary assessment. These assessments should not be shared with other members of the class, but they help students put their drafts into perspective with regard to overall quality. The following rubric is easy for students to use.

Preliminary Assessment

Quality	Assessment
Spelling, grammar, and vocabulary are perfectly correct.	= 4
The majority of the spelling, grammar, and vocabulary is correct.	= 3
About half of the spelling, grammar, and vocabulary is correct.	= 2
Less than half of the spelling, grammar, and vocabulary is correct.	= 1
Almost none of the spelling, grammar, and vocabulary is correct.	= 0

Step 13: Rewrite

Using the information that they receive from their peers, students now revise their drafts. Instead of simply having them make the corrections indicated, encourage students to clarify or emphasize the overall message.

Phase 4: Assessing

Step 14: Assess

Many teachers dislike teaching writing because it is time consuming and the evaluation process can be excruciating. In our experience, we found that correcting or coding grammar and spelling errors is counterproductive. Therefore, we like to use a simple holistic rubric that focuses on comprehensibility as well as accuracy. After the self-editing and peer-editing steps, this type of assessment is usually sufficient.

Scale for Evaluating Compositions

Score	Comprehensibility
50	Message totally comprehensible
40	Majority of message comprehensible
30	About half of message comprehensible
20	Less than half of message comprehensible
10	Message almost totally incomprehensible
0	Message totally incomprehensible

Score	Accuracy
50	Grammar, spelling, punctuation almost completely accurate
40	Majority of grammar, spelling, punctuation accurate
30	About half of grammar, spelling, punctuation accurate
20	Less than half of grammar, spelling, punctuation accurate
10	Grammar, spelling, punctuation almost totally inaccurate
0	Grammar, spelling, punctuation totally inaccurate

Scoring compositions:

____Comprehensibility (effectiveness of communication, content, vocabulary)

____Accuracy (control of grammar, spelling, punctuation)

____Total

The Time Factor

How long does the step-by-step approach take? In our experience, the following schedule has proven effective. For classes that meet five days per week, the complete writing cycle for a major composition takes one and one half weeks. Remember that the instructor completes Step 14. The amount of time needed for assessment depends on class size, teaching load, and many other factors.

	Day 1	Day 2	Day 3	Day 4	Day 5	Day 6	Days 7--
In class	1-2-3	4-5	6-7	8			
At home				9	10-11	12-13	14

At the beginning of this article, we stated that developing good writing skills takes time and practice. Writing practice can take many forms–not only major compositions but also shorter writing tasks completed in class or at home. We have tried the following tasks at different times with good success:

• Daily journals. Dialogue journals, which require the teacher to correspond with students, are very time consuming. However, our experience shows that the daily act of writing short journal entries has a positive overall effect on writing skills, even when teachers do not dialogue with their students.

- News briefs. Having students watch, listen to, or read news from Spanish-speaking countries and then summarize the events in "news brief" format, is an excellent writing task. Countries may be assigned or self-selected. Teachers can call on a different student each day to report briefly on the most interesting news item that she/he found, thereby extending a writing task to incorporate oral practice.

- Personal perspectives (**A mi manera**). Taking the chapter theme as a point of departure, students present their personal perspectives in the form of a paragraph-length writing task. Postcards, a favorite activity, a strange thing that happened, and other topics can be assigned on a frequent basis. A typical chapter theme provides multiple topics for such writing tasks. These short assignments can also be expanded into longer compositions. Appendix A lists several short writing tasks.

We have found that it is not necessary (or possible) to collect and grade all writing tasks. Thorough assessment should be reserved for longer writing assignments, like those outlined in our step-by-step approach. Shorter writing tasks do not always need to be graded. Keeping students on task, however, requires innovative techniques like the following:

- Collect a manageable amount of written work each day (1-5 students), read it, and comment briefly on content and accuracy. Do not make corrections or code errors. Over the course of the semester, quarter, or grading period, you will have collected at least one writing sample from every student.

- Have students keep their writing assignments in a separate notebook which they hand in once or twice during the term. Flip through each notebook to determine whether a reasonable effort has been made (the "eyeball" test) and whether the student merits credit or no credit. You may wish to collect notebooks from half the class at a time to avoid having to carry a large load of notebooks to your office.

- Call on individual students to read their writing assignments in class and ask other students questions about the content. During a typical quarter or semester, every student should be able to read aloud at least once.

Conclusion

We find that this step-by-step approach to teaching is effective because it focuses on planning, requires that students produce multiple versions of a writing task, and incorporates self, peer, and teacher assessment. Although the first three phases (planning, writing, and revising) move slowly, the final assessment phase can be completed quickly by using a simple rubric.

References

Conde, R. (1999). El muerte. In D.R. Long and J.L. Macián. *De paseo*, 2nd ed. (p. 302). Boston: Heinle & Heinle.

Flower, L., & Hayes, J.R. (1981). A cognitive process theory of writing. *College composition and communication, 32,* 365-387.

Gaudiani, C. (1981). *Teaching writing in the foreign language curriculum.* Language in education: Theory and practice (vol. 43). Washington, DC: Center for Applied Linguistics.

Krashen, S. (1984). *Writing: Research, theory, and application.* Oxford: Pergamon Press.

Landeros, T. (2000). Patizza Jiménez se atreve a escribir acerca de la anorexia. *Etylo*, March/April, 77.

Magnan, S.(1985).Teaching and testing proficiency in writing: Skills to transcend the second-language classroom. In A. Omaggio (Ed.) *Proficiency, curriculum, articulation: The ties that bind* (pp. 109-136). Middlebury, VT: Northeast Conference on the Teaching of Foreign Languages.

Ohio ESL.(August 15, 2000). *The Writing Process.* Available: http://www.ohiou.edu/esl/english/writing/process.html.

Richards, J. (1990). *The language teaching matrix.* Cambridge: Cambrige University Press.

Scott, V.M. (1996). *Rethinking foreign language writing.* Boston: Heinle & Heinle.

Shrum, J.L., & Glisan, E.W. (1994). *Teachers' handbook: Contextualized language instruction.* Boston: Heinle & Heinle.

Appendix A: Short Writing Tasks

Notes and post cards

- Welcome to the university (school vocabulary, "study" verbs)
- Self-introduction (action verbs, descriptive adjectives)
- A letter from the year 2050/What did you do to improve the planet (ecology vocabulary; imperfect, preterit)
- Persuasion (ecology, organ donation, politics, etc., subjunctive, commands, expressions of obligation)
- Recommendations (subjunctive, commands)
- Travel (action verbs, hotel vocabulary, places, preterit)

Short journal entries

- My best friend (comparison/contrast)
- My routine (reflexive pronouns)
- My family (descriptive adjectives, family vocabulary)
- My dwelling (gustar, house vocabulary, prepositions of location)
- My household chores (house vocabulary, action verbs)
- My hero (descriptive adjectives)
- My favorite clothes (clothing vocabulary, fabrics, colors, styles, reflexive pronouns)
- My job (action verbs, workplace vocabulary)
- Family activities in the past (pastimes, imperfect, preterit)
- My plans for _____ (future tense)
- My current activities (activities, venues, action verbs)
- A recipe (foods, measurements, commands)

7
Teamwork in Exploring the Target Culture: Creating a Foreign Language Newspaper

Sydney Norton
University of Southern Indiana

Introduction

This article is a synthesis and analysis of teaching experiences drawn from the "The German Press," a third-year course required of all German majors and minors at the University of Southern Indiana (USI).[1] Focusing primarily on the creation of an issue of a foreign language newspaper, the paper presents the techniques and strategies that make the course a unique and worthwhile experience for both students and language teachers. Four fundamental components of the course will be outlined that culminate in the making of the newspaper. Further, the discussion will demonstrate how the activities of each course component serve as an effective tool for developing valuable linguistic and communicative skills that remain with language students long after the course has ended. The press course is unique in four fundamental areas: (1) High-intermediate and advanced language students familiarize themselves with a variety of newspapers, magazines, and news programs from the target culture. Through discussions of articles and news documentaries, they become better informed of current events in the diverse realms of politics, social development, literature, music, and art in the target culture(s). (2) Through directed analysis of a variety of journalistic styles, students substantially expand their vocabulary, while simultaneously mastering more advanced grammatical constructions present in journalistic writing. (3) Students implement their newfound knowledge of current events and simultaneously stretch their linguistic capabilities to their highest potential by writing copy on subjects that interest them most. (4) Students apply their knowledge of the target language in a realistic setting. By working together as part of an editorial staff, class members draw upon skills that extend beyond those of language learning; they learn to appreciate the value of teamwork.

Component I: Choice of Text, Vocabulary Building, and Exams

Teaching a press course can be a uniquely rewarding learning experience in that it differs notably from language and literature courses regularly taught in language programs. In most language and literature courses, students work either with a single textbook and accompanying materials or a group of literary works that the instructor has pre-selected before the semester begins. A press course, however, allows the teacher to develop the the curriculum with the students' contributions, with their selection of momentous current events that they want to write about. The course content is, therefore, automatically tailored to the personal interests of both students and instructor. There are numerous extant textbooks dedicated to the topic of "the press" that teachers can use in class to work through difficult grammatical concepts present in journalistic writing such as indirect speech, participial and passive constructions. However, the most engaging and thought provoking texts are articles chosen from current issues of magazines and newspapers in the target language. *Stern, Der Spiegel, Focus, Die Zeit, Frankfurter Allgemeine* contain a wealth of current information on political events, domestic affairs, and social developments, while pieces from less sophisticated publications such as *Bild, Brigitte, Freundin, Sport* provide a welcome respite from denser, linguistically and intellectually more challenging texts. The "lighter" stories that appear in illustrated newspapers and magazines provide ample opportunity to analyze elements of sensationalism, and to compare them to those of the home culture. These articles, together with cartoons about politics and social life provide more accessible humor for language students and offer, in combination with the "serious" articles discussed in class, a more realistic representation of the diversity of press languages and methods of reporting.

In order to enhance students' vocabulary to its fullest, each assigned article is distributed with approximately thirty underlined words, the understanding of which is crucial for optimal comprehension of the article. A list of definitions of the underlined words accompanies each article. Students are responsible for memorizing these words and for demonstrating that they know what they mean by creating sentences that reveal their comprehension of each word. During the course of the semester, three 50-minute exams are administered that cover all selected vocabulary as well as particular grammatical structures practiced in class. The tests are straightforward in the respect that sentences are duplicated from the article and require students to fill in the missing vocabulary. Thus, students prepare for the test by reading and re-reading the articles discussed in class until they have mastered the new words and understand them in context. Simultaneously they are further engaging themselves with the cultural content of the article. This kind of test preparation helps students expand their word power while acquiring greater insight into the target culture. Class discussions that deal with the article's subject matter help students draw comparisons between the target culture and their own.

Component II: News Documentaries and Video Journalism

While the reading and discussion of current articles can best be conducted in a traditional classroom setting, the remainder of the press course should, if possible, be carried out in the language lab. A fundamental aspect of the course is to familiarize students with spoken journalistic language of the target culture. This goal can best be achieved by analyzing the language and content of brief news clips lasting no more than three to five minutes. A particularly useful resource for teachers of German is *Deutschlandspiegel,* a monthly series put out by the German Information Center that contains four or five brief but culturally rich documentaries on various news items that span the realms of economics, performing arts, social questions, and politics.[2] Since the spoken language is often surprisingly fast for students, the video is usually shown first without sound, asking students what they think the documentary is about, and brainstorming about the probable subject matter. Before showing the video a second time with sound, a number of words are introduced that are fundamental to the understanding of the text. Following the second showing, three to five content questions are distributed based on the documentary. Students listen to the documentary a third time, break up into groups and answer the questions. Following a class discussion, the script is distributed, containing the underlined words and definitions students are expected to memorize. Presenting and discussing a five-minute video once or twice per week has a tremendous accumulative effect on students in terms of language comprehension. Regular work with news clips helps students to develop their interpretive linguistic skills as well as to gain further knowledge and understanding of the target culture.

Component III: From Readership to Creative Production

About halfway through the semester, after reading and discussing numerous diverse articles and news clips, students switch from the role of intelligent reader and listener to that of active and inquisitive reporter. It is helpful at this point to pass around a list of all articles discussed in class and have students sign up for topics on which they would like to do further research. If students have a particular interest in a topic not covered in class–music, the performing arts, painting, sports–they are welcome to research that story. This is the first concrete step toward creating the language newspaper. It is also a time when students should be investigating events related to the target culture that are taking place on campus and in the community. Interviewing an exchange student or native speaker of the target language living in the community is always a culturally rewarding and challenging activity.

During Fall Semester 1998, the USI Foreign Language Program designed a month-long colloquium entitled *Germany in US*. During this time, German Press students interviewed and videotaped visiting scholars from Germany as well as German speaking scholars and musicians from the community who participated in the colloquium. One student with a double major in art and German attended a lecture on German art. His previous knowledge of art history combined with his interest in the subject matter of the lecture resulted in a sophisticated and insightful review that was published in the newspaper. Other students paired up to interview and videotape the colloquium's distinguished speaker from Germany who spoke about the economic relationship between the United States and Germany, while others followed the story of a German POW artist who painted murals at Camp Breckenridge. All interviews were published in the newspaper and they enjoyed substantial readership by German speaking readers otherwise not involved in the press course. The creative element of the press course helped students transcend the structural framework of the standard university course, and enabled them to implement both communicative and foreign language skills, in order to enrich and inform their community.

Component IV: The Newspaper

One of the advantages of living in the computer age is having access to software that allows instructors and students to create without having to worry about the mechanics of the actual production process. A publishing software program enables students to organize text and graphics, insert photos, experiment with numerous fonts, and to enhance the layout by inserting captions, a table of contents, and special features. The existence of user-friendly publishing software frees up a tremendous amount of time that can in turn be channeled into the most exciting component of the press course; language students working together as part of an editorial staff. The final month of the course consists of students' working in the language lab with minimal guidance from the instructor, pulling all of their articles, reviews, opinion pieces, photos, and cartoons into an engaging, well organized and visually appealing newspaper. Class members nominate and then vote on a responsible Editor in Chief. Students whose talents are appropriate for the task fill the remainder of the editorial staff positions. Those interested in art design are in charge of graphics and layout; gifted grammarians become editors and proofreaders. Photography buffs become photographers and photo editors. The computer student will enjoy being in charge of maintaining the newspaper on a central computer, saving a hard copy of the work, and creating a web site for the newspaper.

A week before the end of the semester, members of the press course hand in their final copy, and the instructor provides a final reading. While the instructor is proofing, it is crucial that he or she not attempt to change or edit students' ideas, but rather concentrate on catching overlooked grammatical errors and misspellings. Final copy goes to employees of media services who make a hundred or so copies of the issue. The last day of class, students receive a hard copy of their newspaper and a handful of copies to distribute to all other German speakers in the community. The foreign language newspaper is a tribute to a semester of linguistic challenges, cultural immersion, creativity, and fun.

Notes

[1]   Many of the conclusions drawn in this paper, as well as some of the teaching strategies articulated, derive from valuable discussions with my colleague Donald Wolfe, who conceived the "German Press" and taught the course for many years.

[2]   While a comparable monthly news video may not be available to French, Spanish, and Japanese teachers, downloading and recording daily news programs off of the Internet or taping news programs from television fulfills the same function. It is, of course, necessary to carefully preview this material by making sure that students are introduced to unfamiliar vocabulary.

8

Language Learning and Cultural Adjustment: Information and Implications for ESL/Foreign Language Instructors

Lisa M. Calvin
Indiana State University

Language learners who study abroad may anticipate that an immersion experience will aid language acquisition, and that living in a new culture certainly will be a personally enriching experience. But life in the target language culture (TLC) often leads to culture shock (CS), which diverts attention and energy from learning the second language (L2) (Schumann, 1975). This ethnographic case study represents an exploration into the simultaneous processes of language learning and cross-cultural adaptation, as self-reported by adult ESL students in a private language school.[1] The first section of the present report examines the ways in which students experienced symptoms of culture shock and anxiety issues related to their adjustment, including the role of critical incidents in student motivation. The second section addresses strategies used by learners to cope with adaptation and to learn the language. Based on the findings, the report includes a discussion of pedagogical implications.[2]

Cultural Adaptation

Phase One of Cultural Adaptation: Symptoms of Culture Shock

Of the symptoms that Kohls lists for "relatively severe cases of culture shock" (1979, p.65), the researcher identified evidence of the following symptoms in the learning journal entries of students at the language school: the need for excessive amounts of sleep, homesickness, boredom, withdrawal, concern about cleanliness, unexplainable fits of weeping, and a change in work effectiveness.

Tiredness

Particularly in the first week, but throughout the stay, students wrote about their tiredness, *"The first week is finish and my head is full with english, a new land, new people. I feel me tired. –Beate "*[3] Adjustment to a new language and culture can be exhausting, as Beate's entries related, but need not be a harbinger of CS. However, statements of tiredness can announce the possibility of further symptoms as evidenced through observation and journals. For even when learners demonstrate no signs of CS, tiredness could nevertheless immediately impact students' academic pursuits, influencing motivation, as Helene's case below.

Homesickness

Some students applied the label "homesick" to the emotion that they were experiencing, others felt "lonely," and still others simply talked nostalgically about people from home without knowing what they were experiencing. Helene wrote, *"Last week I had a little crisis. One thing was, that I felt physical[l]y not good. I had a little cold and a cold sore on my lips. The other was, that I felt lonely. I thought that all people had forgotten [me]. I felt lost in spit[e] of all the people around me. I have seen that many people had the same problem."* Addressing homesickness quickly and individually may help counter a contagious effect. Such was not the case with one woman in the program whose feelings of loneliness left her reduced to tears for over a week, creating a wave of homesickness among other learners.

Boredom

Only one key informant, Yoon Soo, expressed the CS symptom of boredom. One of his hobbies in Korea had been playing billiards, and since he could not play in the TLC because the serving of alcohol conflicted with his religious beliefs, he wrote that his life now was boring. Upon return from two school field trips, Yoon Soo described the trips as boring, comparing the sites negatively to his home culture. For example, in Yoon Soo's opinion, hiking in a nearby national park was boring because in Korea one could climb "real" mountains. As in this case, the use of "boring" as a catch-all word may mask other symptoms such as homesickness and feelings of nationalism.

Withdrawal

The CS symptom of withdrawal can be a psychological reaction difficult to observe as well as a physical separation that is partially observable. Because of the numerical strength of the Korean home culture group at the school in this study, most Korean students spent their free time together speaking in Korean, withdrawing from the host culture and other ESL students.

Concern for Cleanliness

Kohls (1979) describes the tendency of Americans abroad to become obsessive about standards of cleanliness, but such attitudes and behavior are not limited to Americans. For example, one particularly striking example of cultural adjustment for Yoon Soo was his disgust and dismay at the Western method of washing dishes in an increasingly dirty dishpan of water.

Change in Work Habits

Other ESL students who demonstrated symptoms of severe CS, lamented their loss of productivity. "I don't know what's wrong with me. I'm not usually like this. I usually work very hard," was a typical comment punctuating this phase of adaptation. Katrin, a key informant from Switzerland who felt that life in another Western culture required no adjustment for her, nevertheless echoed these same sentiments regarding a change in her normal study habits. Normally so studious that she felt it bordered obsession, Katrin found the change a pervasive and bothersome peculiarity throughout her stay. This reaction suggests that the loss of ability to work effectively may be a stage in the progression toward CS, but not all who experience it necessarily advance to a severe stage of CS. In addition to teaching learning strategy tips, instructors may wish to remind students of basic study habits to counteract the ill effects of this phase of CS.

Phase Two of Cultural Adaptation: Adjustment Issues

According to CS theory, the CS phase is followed by an adjustment phase. Whether actually experiencing CS or not, those abroad undergo an adjustment that is not limited to culture and that may include some degree of anxiety. Hilleson (1996) used diary study and interview methods to determine which language learning factors lead to debilitating anxiety. For the purpose of categorizing learners' experiences in the present study, Hilleson's model incorporating three types of adjustment-related categories is helpful: (1) language shock; (2) foreign language anxiety; and (3) classroom anxiety. A fourth category of *outside influences* is introduced in the present research.

Language Shock

Mirroring the principles of CS yet focusing upon language, the notion of language shock suggests that anxiety is caused by a move to an environment in which one's native language is no longer the language of interaction or instruction (Hilleson). Diary comments related to self-perception, facilitating and debilitating anxiety, reactions to total immersion, and the transition period would be categorized as language shock.

Self-perception, Anxiety, Immersion

The following journal entries trace a gemeral informant's struggles with identity change, feelings of stupidity, and efforts to manage anxiety. This Korean learner's stress management during a difficult time included encouraging self-talk, goal setting, and prayer. She writes:

> —*Originally I am a talkative and serious girl. I like to talk with people and to play. But I changed a lot, if I am school, I become a shy girl. I don't speak [to] another person particular[ly] foreigners because I can't speak English well. Mentally I feel daunted. Sometime I am like idiot. I can use short sentences, easy words. That's all!*

> —*I am under a lot of stress but I hope that I could gain the great fruits in English. Education is difficult but very important. I will study English hard. Fight, Eun Ju! 11/10*

> —*Tests, homeworks, journals, conversation etc. I am under a lot of stress because of English nowadays. To learn a foreign language is very difficult and hard. Many times a day, I asked myself, "Do I must do it?" But I myself answered "Sure." Nowadays I can't express ideas, thought and feelings to my heart's contents beacuse I must speak not Korean but English. Oh, my God? Please help me. Help me. 11/15*

> —*Nowadays I've feeled so tired because of bad cough. I become weak and I am worn. I am sad. I wept and wept. 11/24*

Eun Ju's words such as "daunted," "idiot," "stress," and "wept" poignantly capture the psychological turmoil of CS and the language shock of not being able to express herself and sensing an identity change. She had changed from being talkative to being shy. The journal dates are indicative of the gradual, progressive nature of CS, which in this case culminated in fits of weeping. Negative feelings of ignorance potentially could lead to raising the affective filter and furthering the onset of debilitating anxiety for language learners.

Language Transition Period

The present research documents two phases of the language transition phase that can cause distress for students. One is identified as *reaching a plateau* in which a learner senses he or she is making no progress and expresses feelings of linguistic stagnation. In an interview, about halfway through the language program, the third key informant, Ana, discussed such feelings. In both journal entries and one-on-one interviews, learners in this study discussed concerns about their linguistic plateau but did not elaborate as to whether they felt it led to debilitating or facilitating anxiety.

During another part of the language transition phase, the learner is still processing the vast amount of cognitive input and feels overwhelmed. According to this respondent, her *overly active conscious monitor* (Schumann, 1978) during this phase led to hesitant speech production.

— *"I wish I could stay here for a longer time. I feel that I am in a phase (with my english) where I have problems to speak, because I am afraid to make mistakes. I can understand much, but I am confused with all the knowledge, that I can't use yet. –Helene."*

This statement suggests that while formal instruction may ultimately benefit the learner, she may pass through a brief phase in which use of the monitor has negative results.

Foreign Language Anxiety

In Hilleson's study, the second type of debilitating anxiety identified is foreign language anxiety, an anxiety induced by the need to perform tasks in an unfamiliar language. In Eun Ju's journal entry above, there is evidence that language shock was exacerbated by the classroom tasks required. Yoon Soo compared his present immersion experience to previous ones and, comparatively, felt that he suffered little from CS at the language school. Instead of the symptoms of CS, his journal was peppered with comments about stress from speaking English. He discussed this language anxiety in interviews, commenting, *"[I am so nervous about] this sentence, so I can't understand [the] next sentence...so I have some stress."* He found this problem particularly debilitating and frustrating with discussion topics in which he believed he was an expert but could not share content knowledge for lack of linguistic knowledge.

Classroom Anxiety: Importance of a Shared Belief

Hilleson's (1996) third category for data analysis, classroom anxiety, relates to performance expectations within the L2 classroom and in academic activities. In the language school context studied, discussions of classroom anxiety are conspicuously absent. In interviews with Katrin and Ana, they stressed the importance of a being in a religious context for lowering affective concerns. Ana felt that, in such an environment, others would not laugh at her. The Christian school's approach of reaching "the mind and the heart," as Katrin expressed it, appealed to her. Katrin felt that beginning the school day with an all-school meditation period modeled the idea of unity, which in turn fostered a cooperative-versus-competitive atmosphere in the classroom. Students attributed the close student-student and student-teacher relations to the Christian atmosphere.

That this Christian context reduced the anxiety of some learners is evident from the data; whether that reduction also explains the lack of student discussions about classroom anxiety is uncertain.

Outside Influence on Adjustment and Learning

Anxiety from Outside Factors

Although collected data showed no evidence of students experiencing Hilleson's third category of debilitating anxiety, journal entries suggest a fourth debilitating category: anxiety from outside forces. Katrin and Ana both discussed reduced motivation after receiving letters from home that contained bad news. For Ana the news that lack of funding might terminate her study abroad experience created great anxiety that influenced her attendance and academic work.

Critical Incidents

The role of encounters perceived as negative cross-cultural clashes, or critical incidents, can influence motivation for social integration with the TLC and thus the cultural adjustment and language learning process of the learner. According to CS theory, CS is a gradual process, and no one incident solely triggers it (Kohls, 1979). However, the researcher learned from conversations with respondents that negative experiences with native speakers had indeed facilitated or debilitated the motivation of the learner. Thus, one social incident influenced a long-term affective response.

An incident can be so negatively perceived that a learner decides to discontinue language learning, while for another learner the negative incident may serve as a defining moment in motivating language study. For example, during an interview with Ana, she told of a negative incident which served as a defining moment in her motivation. Using the internalized assumptions of her Brazilian culture, Ana interpreted the lack of eye contact in the TLC as an unwillingness to speak to her and a personal rejection. She assumed that the rejection was a result of her inability to speak English, and consequently she vowed to learn the language well and was more motivated to learn than when she had left home.

Student Strategies for Adjustment and Learning

Coping Strategies

Since the publication of Oxford's (1990) seminal work in language learning strategies, research has burgeoned in this field. And just as learners utilize and develop strategies to help them deal with the task of language learning, similarly the learners in this study developed strategies to deal with the stresses of cross-cultural adjustment during the language learning process.

Relaxation Strategies

The two key coping strategies used by general informants were relaxation techniques: *meditating in a natural setting* and *socializing with other learners.* Asians and Westerners mention walks along the nearby beach as a coping strategy when stressed, or as one student put it, *"my head began to smoke."*

Despite a supportive community of L2 speakers, at times, only a break from L2 and a return to speaking L1 with other students could relieve the pressure. Luther's entry indicates that part of the reason for a switch to L1 was to communicate at a depth beyond his proficiency level in English, *"I am sure this conversation would be not possible for us in english-language. And so I am glad, that we were only german-language-speaking people, because I need sometimes deep conversations."*

Religious Strategies

To deal with cultural adaptation, the three key informants, who used different language learning strategies, were strikingly similar in their use of cultural coping strategies. All three used music for encouragement and relaxation, with Ana emphasizing the English lyrics in religious music. Yoon Soo listened to Christian music in L1. Each learner drew upon another source of spiritual encouragement. Ana used her daily reading of the Bible as an encouragement strategy. Katrin noted the use of prayer to help her cope. Yoon Soo stated that he was able to cope because of the encouragement he received in knowing that friends at home were praying for him.

Various Personal Strategies

The few other coping strategies used by Katrin and Yoon Soo were non-religious in nature. Katrin arranged her schedule to allow for time alone each day. Arranged solitude was also a practical learning strategy for Katrin because she was not able to study with the constant chatter at the school. She also employed positive self-talk to cope. Yoon Soo played a variety of sports to reduce his stress.

Student learning journals can provide insight, for language teachers in immersion settings, into the possible onset of CS feelings and the anxieties of adjustment. While journal topics may be open-ended, instructors may wish to ask guided questions to uncover affective issues and to provide cultural perspectives which could help offset the negativity of critical incidents.

Further Pedagogical Implications

The Importance and Role of Music

Vocabulary and Pronunciation

Music is an essential element in the language teaching method Suggestopedia, but this study indicates that student-generated rather than teacher-imposed music can also play an important role in language learning. In Oxford's (1990) taxonomy of strategies, listening to music before performing an activity is categorized as affective, but student respondents in the present study reported linguistic benefits of listening to music, thus broadening Oxford's use. First, vocal music has the linguistic benefits of lexical acquisition and a focus on pronunciation. It can be used formally in the classroom as well as informally on group excursions during travel by bus or van.

Communication and Bonding

Second, music serves as a topic for communicative exchanges and promotes group bonding. In the present study, discussion of songs provided an impetus for communication in informal settings. Following one field trip, several students, including a novice learner who rarely spoke, conversed about songs sung in their home churches. Throughout the study, the researcher observed that music commonly generated this bonding effect upon the group. During free time, students gravitated toward the conference room where instruments were kept. Music joined cultures, with Brazilian and German guitarists accompanying a Korean keyboardist and American and British vocalists providing the lyrics.

Cross-cultural Understanding

Third, students demonstrated growth in metacultural awareness and an increase in cross-cultural understanding through music. Students demonstrated an acceptance of other cultures and an appreciation for other languages by learning to sing songs in peers' L1 and listening to peers' musical cassettes in L1.

Coping Strategy

Fourth, music was used as a coping strategy to lower learner anxiety. Four days after Eun Ju's previously cited journal entries, the tearful student in the midst of an identity crisis found solace through inspirational music. Encouraged, she wrote, *"I sang a song." 'I don't know about tomorrow, I just live from day to day. Many things about tomorrow, I don't seem to understand. But I know who holds tomorrow, and I know who holds my hand.' What an amazing song it is! 11/28."*

Use of Multiple Intelligences

Finally, Howard Gardner (1983) has proposed that musical ability is a different kind of "intelligence" than linguistic intelligence. Therefore, providing opportunities for the integration of music may allow some students to excel in one intelligence while struggling in the language area. Talent shows or "fun night" activities sponsored by language programs could be entertaining as well as intellectually stimulating events.

The Meeting of Religion, the State, and the Language Learner

The separation of church and state in American public education, not-withstanding the variety of religions generally represented in academic L2 learning contexts, makes impossible a unified religious context as was experienced by the learners of this study. However, this limitation need not suggest that religious language students uniquely be directed toward like-minded institutions in order to achieve a lowered anxiety level, as highlighted by the learners in the present study reported a lowered anxiety level because they knew that their teachers and peers shared the same religion.

Discussing in Written and Oral Communication

Without promoting religion, language educators can exhibit a receptivity to learning about any values, perspectives, holidays, and traditions of the home culture, including those of a religious nature. This receptivity could include explicitly granting students permission to write about topics of a spiritual or religious nature in journals or compositions. Additionally teachers might ask students to contrast the perceived differences of religion in daily life in the home and host cultures. Communicating to overtly religious students that their religious values are esteemed, rather than treating religion as taboo, may open up the lines of communication.

The original journal assignment for this study focused on language and culture, but when students expanded the assignment to include issues of a spiritual nature, the communication was expanded in the form of increased length of journal entries. For example, at the outset, Yoon Soo's entries were 4-5 lines in length, and by the third through eighth week of the study, he was composing entries of 6-8 lines in length. Yet from the beginning, Yoon Soo wrote 12-19 line entries when writing about a spiritually-related issue. When writing in his journal about his spiritual journey before he came to the language school, Yoon Soo wrote two and a half pages of narrative.

Building the Reading Collection.

Library and classroom collections could be built to include religious titles, thus demonstrating openness to spiritual concerns as well as providing literature of interest for students who have background knowledge in this topic.

Creating Informal Learning Areas

A family atmosphere, which informants attributed to the Christian context, can be created in other learning environments. For adult learners, the establishment of teacher-student lounges or coffee rooms may help to create an informal, familial atmosphere that produces affective and linguistic benefits.

Conclusion

Through language learning stories told by a few students, rich insight into the simultaneous processes of language learning and cross-cultural adaptation has been gained. The first step in helping students cope with immersion anxieties is to diagnosis the problem; the second is to provide them with strategies for coping with the negative effects of CS; and the third is to improve the learning context to optimize learning.

Notes

[1]   The study involves the development of case study profiles of three key informants: a Brazilian, a Korean, and a Swiss-German adult in a 12-week intensive English program (IEP). Using a qualitative approach, the researcher adopted a position of participant observer and used multiple data collection and analysis techniques. These included language learning journals, administrative documents, learner assignments, ongoing observation, a questionnaire on strategy use, five taped interviews for each key informant, shadowing of participants, peer debriefing, member checks, prolonged on-site engagement, and researcher's log. Although this inner circle served as the core for the information gathered, all other students in the two intermediate classes were general informants who wrote learning journals and were observed in group settings.

[2]   The theoretical implications discussed at the Central States Conference can be read in Calvin (1999). Readers interested in knowing more of students' poignant stories of cross-cultural adaptation and language victories are encouraged to read that document. See references.

[3]   All quotes from journals use pseudonyms of language school students in the study.

References

Calvin, L. M. (1999). *Culture within and around language learning stories of adults in a cross-cultural, instructional immersion setting.* Unpublished doctoral dissertation, Indiana University, Bloomington.

Gardner, H. (1983). *Frames of mind: The theory of multiple intelligences.* New York: Basic Books.

Hilleson, M. (1996). 'I want to talk with them, but I don't want them to hear': An introspective study of L2 anxiety in an English-medium school. In K. M. Bailey and D. Nunan (Eds.), *Voices from the language classroom: qualitative research in second language education* (pp. 248-275). New York: Cambridge.

Kohls, R. (1979). *Survival kit for overseas living.* Chicago: Intercultural Press, Inc.

Oxford, R. (1990). *Language learning strategies.* New York: Newbury House.

Schumann, J. H. (1975). Affective factors and the problem of age in second language acquisition. *Language Learning, 25,* 209-235.

Schumann, J. H. (1978). The acculturation model for second language acquisition. In R. C. Gingras (Ed.), *Second language acquisition and foreign language teaching* (pp. 27-50). Washington, DC: Center for Applied Linguistics.

9
Playing with a Purpose: Defining the Issues

John I. Liontas
University of Notre Dame

Introduction[1]

Since the dark ages of education, games have always been utilized by educators as tools for instruction and entertainment. Their very presence in all aspects of human life throughout time–from antiquity to today–strongly suggests the intrinsic value so many of us place upon them. While it remains an indisputable fact that part of their appeal lies in the entertainment value they provide, a great many of us in the language teaching profession employ games precisely because we are convinced that their use adds a new dimension to second language learning: *purposeful learning.*

It is this type of learning that is the focus of this article. It is neither intended to cover the different types of games available for language teaching (i.e., crossword puzzles, word-search puzzles, scrambled word games, board games, card games, computer games, etc.) nor to discuss the developmental framework of proficiency-based game approaches for language instruction; the latter has been adequately addressed elsewhere (Liontas, 1992a, 1992b; Omaggio, 1978, 1982; Siskin & Spinelli, 1987). It is, however, the intention of this article to take a closer look at the type of learning that can occur as a result of using games (used here in the broadest sense) to achieve a set of predetermined linguistic and sociocultural curricular ends. Following a brief review of the type of learning one should engender in the second language classroom, this article then suggests two time-tested game formats that over the years have found wide appeal among both secondary and post-secondary second language learners.

Going Beyond Fun and Games

By design, games are intended to heighten the element of fun, and some of them achieve this more readily than others. But is "fun" alone enough reason to employ a game in the language classroom? For example, a game like *Mensch ärgere dich nicht!* (*Parcheesi* ™) loved by many generations of German children and parents alike, may well score a ten on the "fun" scale, but will undoubtedly score very low on a learning scale measuring linguistic or sociocultural progress in the target language. Aside from the occasional reaction of joy to one's own or the other player's roll of the die, very little measurable linguistic output is generated as a result of playing this game. It is not suggested that this game fulfills no immediate purpose, for I still enjoy this game and play it to this day with friends and family. As a language educator, however, I find it difficult to justify to myself and other educators the use of this game during regular class time other than perhaps for exposing students to the types of games that my family and others in the German-speaking world would play. Exposing students to the games the people of the target culture play is a valid goal of language teaching and, furthermore, it does address at least two of the five Cs listed in the *Standards for Foreign Language Learning* (1996): culture and comparisons.

But, exposure alone, even when coupled with the element of fun, should not drive the language curriculum, at least not the one envisaged here. Instead, the driving force behind a game's use during class time should be the language quality, not quantity, generated as a result. Said another way: Are students' aural, oral, written, or reading skills and knowledge of culture better now than before the introduction of this game? Does this game promote or complement that which is being learned in the classroom or does it only release tension from the day-to-day responsibilities of language teaching and learning? Without a doubt, the latter is a "necessary evil" in language instruction, but it is the former that should command closer scrutiny by language professionals today. With ever-increasing curricular demands placed upon teachers by boards of education, departments, schools, and communities, the scrutiny of the question "To Play or Not to Play?" weighs more heavily in the minds of many.

Consequently, the question before us is not whether we should use games or game-like activities, simulations, and approaches in our language teaching and learning (Buehler, 1979; Danesi, 1987; Hacken, 1979; Lynch, 1986; Wright, 1989) but, rather, entertainment values aside, which learning values are being sought within (and beyond) the target language classroom. It follows that the purpose and the potential benefit of the game chosen to meet specific instructional ends need to be made clear to students, administrators, parents, and teachers. The argument that clothes this article is a simple one, albeit challenging at times: *Play should have a pur-*

pose (hence the title). What emerges directly from this position are the following questions:

1. How can we be sure that our language learners are playing with a purpose?
2. What constitutes "Playing with a Purpose"?
3. Who determines what the purpose is or should be?
4. How is this purpose best measured and showcased?
5. Why play at all? Are play formats not best left to younger children and avoided with college students or even adult learners?
6. Will my colleagues, administrators, my students' parents, or even my own students take me seriously if they find out that I play games during class time?

It is to these questions that the discussion now turns. There are many ways in which language teachers can ascertain the answers to these questions. Student surveys, focus groups, and mid- and end-of-semester student evaluations are but a few of the ways available to us. Perhaps the most productive way is to involve language learners in the selection, design, and development of a game for instructional purposes. This involvement and the levels of enthusiasm achieved in the utilization of a game are all strong indicators of "Playing with a Purpose." There is no better way to empower language learners than to simply challenge them to (re)invent and produce play-like formats for specific skills and within set parameters of linguistic functions. In all my years of teaching second languages and subjects in a variety of educational settings here and abroad, I have yet to come across learners, young or old, who have not found a way to mesmerize me with their industriousness, creativity, and loyalty to the gaming task at hand. While I am not suggesting that this game-producing process has always been a smooth one, I have nevertheless found this process to be very enlightening and worth pursuing even in adult education.

In this context, it is helpful to bear in mind that the process of (re)inventing a language-learning game–from its inception through the design to the production and application stage–weighs positively on the collaborative environment in which learning ultimately takes place. The resulting learning is not always linear, nor can it be measured concomitantly on a scale of one to ten, as different learners bring different assets to this negotiation process. While the astute instructor must be willing to make some time sacrifices, it is nonetheless very refreshing to see learners transact meaning, propose solutions, offer alternatives, argue points of view, promote collaboration and peer teaching practices, and the like. Depending on class level, much of this type of learning can and should take place in the target language. When coupled with the game's intended linguistic and sociocultural learning, the end result is a powerful one indeed.

Language teachers do not have to reinvent the wheel each and every time game-like learning is called for. Over the course of time, one can amass a number of purposeful games for specific learning goals to be employed with a new class of learners eager to learn (Alsop, 1980; Berman, 1980; Culley, 1986; Smith, 1981). This is not to say that after several semesters there would be no need to create new language-learning games. I have been pleasantly surprised many times in my career when, in game formats that I thought were perfect for what they intended to accomplish, students were able to recommend new twists and ideas to "old" learning games.

Empowering students to determine their own learning with the target language, and the conditions under which this learning is to take place and be measured, should become the common yardstick by which all learning efforts are judged. In short, playing with a purpose means to engage in the same *functions* (communicative tasks), thematic *contents* (interactional topics), and *contexts* (situational settings) in which native speakers use the target language for purposeful communication. Seen under this rubric, games can become an all-empowering vehicle by which the six concerns articulated above win legitimacy in the eyes of students, administrators, parents, and teachers (Hubp, 1974; Kaiser, 1977; Lee, 1979; Schmidt, 1977).

Conversely, playing games in a vacuum without seeking attainment of a specific language objective is as ineffective as embarking on a trip without a known destination. Both the ACTFL Proficiency Guidelines (1986) and, more recently, the *Standards for Foreign Language Learning* (1996) provide language teachers with much needed "traffic signs" along the way to mastering a second language (Lafayette, 1996; Lange, 1999). The local or state curriculum, as well as the language textbook, provide additional arguments for or against the determination of a learning game's purpose. Ultimately, however, it is the students and the teacher who, working together toward a common goal, determine what the purpose of a learning game is or should be. No one knows the dynamics of language learning better than the people responsible for creating them in the first place. And therein lies the greatest strength of playing with a purpose.

I cannot think of a better way to learn another people's language and culture, barring a direct visit to the land, than under the illusion of a game format, while still remaining fully accountable to school boards and administrators for what we teach, how, when, and to whom. With renewed emphasis on testing and performance, accountability has once again moved to the top of the national agenda of politicians and educators. Amidst such intense discussions, it is easy to overlook the many benefits game-like formats, approaches, or simulations offer to both language teachers and students. I will not recite here all the benefits listed in the literature on games for language-learning purposes over the past two decades. This has already been sufficiently addressed elsewhere (Ahmad, 1981; Arnold, 1979; Liontas, 1992a). Suffice it to say, however, that learning games, if planned wisely and used judiciously, can and do become an excellent vehicle by which second language learners can review, practice, and reinforce previously learned classroom material in a fun and entertaining new way. Some of the most important arguments in favor of language-learning games are summarized below.

Why should learning games be used? Because they can...

- Enhance language instruction, they are enjoyable and easy to implement, and they make learning student centered.
- Have outcomes that involve purposeful communication both in comprehension and expression.
- Function as a non teacher-centered medium of language instruction, provide comprehensible linguistic and sociocultural input, and foster personalized communication among learners.
- Be used for drilling, measuring, developing, and bridging a learner's interactive competence and functional language use.
- Ensure more practice time for proficiency, provide ample opportunities for learning, and stimulate active and effective student involvement in self-control, -monitoring, -correction, and -evaluation.
- Adhere to principles of learning while promoting interpersonal, social, and emotional development.
- Stimulate students' interests, promote and increase overt learning, and prolong self-motivation to continue to learn.

Why should language learners engage in the design and application process of learning games? Because through them they can...

- Gain self-confidence, growth, and a sense of accomplishment.
- Engage in meaningful, context-rich learning experiences and tasks that are positive and non-threatening.
- Develop and expand their performance capabilities while generating their own motivation to learn.
- Attain an even greater amount of the cognitive, affective, linguistic, and cultural code of the target language.
- Negotiate meaning, lodge complaints, and accept or decline offers while brainstorming, writing the first draft, and revising and refining the final draft of a game's approach.
- Further their fluency, flexibility, creative skills, and command of the target language.
- Fine-tune their target knowledge both in linguistic usage and cultural appropriateness.
- Sharpen their language sensitivity, enlarge their vocabularies, and expand their idiomatic and cultural understanding.

Why should language teachers include learning games in their repertoire of second language teaching approaches? Because through them they can...

- Promote a peer-supportive, personalized, and anxiety-free atmosphere unlike more conventional language learning experiences.
- Provide themselves with an instructional tool of positive reinforcement to increase, challenge, and stimulate students' motivation, needs, and interests in an unintimidating, cooperative, and relatively anxiety-free learning environment.
- Complement and challenge students' abilities, styles of learning, and levels of proficiency.
- Minimize tension and anxiety during learning.
- Foster ongoing motivation and encourage higher performance from everyone involved.
- Generate and reinforce overt learning behavior relevant to the terminal objectives of the game.
- Revitalize active interaction between groups of learners or individual learners to reach a consensus on games as collaborative problem-solving formats of language learning.

- Legitimize advantages of visibility, sportsmanship, and individualized and collective learning.

More often than not, language-learning games, cloaked in the illusion of "having fun," can become an added teaching tool and informal diagnostic instrument, providing language teachers with a keen sense of their students' rate of retention, ability level, strengths, and weaknesses. Judicious use of games over the course of time provides a much-needed lens by which language learners can project their language growth in a non-threatening, comfortable, and relaxed learning environment–despite the competitive circumstances–while language teachers can measure the overall purpose and success of the learning game employed, making adjustments as needed. At the same time, students' level of participation and enthusiasm during play determines the extent of use of the game in the future. These two variables–level of participation and level of enthusiasm–also determine to a large extent whether a particular game format is best suited to younger children, college students, or even adult learners.

Given these considerations, it must also be emphasized that not all language-learning games are created equal. While some learning games meet the affective and cognitive needs and interests of young learners, the exact same games may well be ill-equipped to do the same for college and adult learners. It is, therefore, imperative that during the design process of a learning game careful consideration be given to the intellectual maturity of the learners involved so that no one feels alienated or even insulted. No less important is the provision of skills progression from one audience to the next. It is strongly advocated here that the best skills progression is one that demands from its designers an ever-increasing level of sophistication as the age and level of performance increases from one group of learners to the next.

Within this progression, it is further advisable that language learners be told well in advance the desired learning outcomes for each game-like activity or simulation as well as the learning behavior, both verbal and non verbal, expected of them at each performance level. This, in turn, legitimizes in the eyes of the students, administrators, parents, and other teachers the choice of games employed during regular class time over other instructional possibilities, thus avoiding the erroneous stigma attached to games as playful devices that waste valuable instructional time.

Playing with a purpose does not mean watering down the language curriculum. On the contrary, it enhances and validates on a daily basis that which is deemed important to second language learning (Crookall & Oxford, 1989; Matheidez, 1988; Wright, Betteridge & Buckby, 1984). Unlike conventional language practices, learning games have the power to bring a fresh air to instructional material long considered cut and dried, while expanding geometrically the opportunities for other types of learning often not even expected in the frantic pace to meet the demands of the language curriculum. A brief account of two such learning games is given in the next section.

A Closer Look at Two Language Learning Games

The two language learning games presented below are part of a larger proficiency-based game approach. Because of space constraints, only their corresponding game boards are described here. These two games have been singled out here because they exemplify how a single game format can address all four language skills and culture while offering learners a multitude of fun and entertainment. Both games require of learners nothing less than their full cooperation in the design and application process. Students begin by brainstorming and writing the material; then they proceed with editing, re-writing, and refining the material, and lastly, they select their best work for inclusion in the finished game board. During play, learners not only have to comprehend what is being said or read but also respond appropriately to each prompt. The conversion of guided intake to pushed output is the hallmark of both games. Both learning games are constructed to be used as a learning tool for the student of German. They have been successfully used since 1986 in college-level German courses as well as at the middle school and high school level and can easily be adapted to other modern languages. In both games the role of the instructor is to serve as a facilitator, coach, and judge of last resort to settle disputes that the student referee(s) cannot resolve.

1. ZOOMANIA

Purpose of Game: To practice critical auditory discrimination and reflective listening while enhancing communicative performance, including figurative competence and cultural knowledge.

Contents: Set of ZOOMANIA cards, one game board card, and 10 to 15 plastic game tokens per player.

Level: First-, second-, and third-year German classes, including elementary learners (with some modification to level of performance).

Number of Players: 2 to 22.

Rules: Each player receives a different game board card (see Figure 1) containing 25 animal fields and 10 to 15 plastic tokens. One student, who serves as the game referee, reads an animal riddle (In ancient Egypt I was regarded as a symbol for luck. According to mythology I have nine lives and I always land on my feet. Who am I?); a simile (You look like a drowned ___); a metaphor (She is a ___); an idiom (To take the ___ by the horns), or a proverb (Don't count your ___ before they're hatched!) from a ZOOMANIA card for all players to hear. Each item card includes the answer (cat, rat, fox, bull, chickens) at the bottom and a designated number in the upper right hand corner. When a player thinks that s/he has solved the riddle, the player shouts "Zoomania" and calls out the number from the game card. If the player's number matches the one the referee has, only then is the student allowed to give the correct answer (loudly and clearly) for the whole class to hear before s/he can place one of the plastic game tokens over the corresponding animal field on the game board card. This approach, in addition to facilitating students' listening comprehension, minimizes opportunities for students to provide wrong responses. The game ends after a player has been able to successfully place 5 game tokens in a row on the playing card (either horizontally, diagonally, or vertically). The first player to do so and yell out "Zoomania" is the winner.

2. BLITZ

Purpose of Game: To practice, review, and reinforce previously learned classroom material while allowing learners to showcase their knowledge of Landeskunde as well as their competence in the target language in general.

Contents: Set of color-coded BLITZ cards, one game board card, and 4 plastic game pieces and 1 die per player/team.

Level: First-, second-, and third-year German classes, including advanced (under) graduate language and adult learners.

Number of Players: Four individuals or four teams (of no more than 4 players per team).

Background: BLITZ the board game, part of the larger game approach to teaching and learning German, is an easy learning game to play and very versatile in its design in that it offers language teachers maximum flexibility in the thematic categories they choose to include depending on learners' age and expected level of performance. Each category is color-coded and corresponds to one of the four color fields present on the game board card: red, yellow, green, and blue. While these colors were selected at random, they do represent, nonetheless, a thematic category. Each thematic category has its own color-coded BLITZ cards and can include virtually anything dealing with the target language and culture from vocabulary items to who wrote which literary work during the second half of the romantic period. The most common categories employed in the past have included Vocabulary Items, Synonyms/Antonyms, Animals, Transportation, Food, Clothing, United States of Europe, German-American Day, Berlin Day, Oktoberfest, Christmas, Karneval (Fasching), Eastern Festivals, Sports, Olympic Games, World Cup Soccer, Famous People, Geography, History, Literature, Poetry, Fairy Tales, Idioms, Proverbs, Fixed Collocations, Riddles, Songs, Horoscope, and the like.

It should be clear from the thematic categories mentioned above that the number of categories could be expanded *ad infinitum*. It should be equally clear that more than one category can have one of the four original field colors. Since more than one category will have the same color, the face of each BLITZ card should be further designated by its theme for quick separation. The back of the card, however, should have no visible markings revealing the theme of the category other than its designated color or a common artistic design pattern. One such pattern is shown in the center of the BLITZ game board card (see Figure 2). This four-color format limits the playing fields to a minimum each time a color field is visited while maximizing the number and variety of thematic categories that can potentially be employed every time this board game is played. As stated above, decisions about which thematic categories are used depend largely upon the age and level of performance desired per play.

Rules: The BLITZ game board card features three learning paths, which the players/teams follow in a clockwise fashion. In turn, each path shows a number of color-coded fields, BLITZ fields, and entry/exit fields, totaling 59 in number. Path 1 includes 28 color-coded fields, of which four are BLITZ fields and four are entry fields into Path 2. With 20 color-coded fields, Path 2 cuts the BLITZ and entry chances in half (two BLITZ fields and two entry fields) while doubling the chances of exiting Path 2. In like manner, the chances of exiting Path 3 with its 11 color-coded fields or hitting a BLITZ field are also cut in half, i.e., one exit field and one BLITZ field respectively. In short, each player/team has seven BLITZ chances, six entry chances, and five exit chances while playing BLITZ. These 18 fields, interspersed strategically through-out the game board card, have been purposely included in this game board in an effort to increase the fun and entertainment value of the learning game. More often than not, these fields become the background of unexpected joy or sheer disappointment and make for some interest-ing body and vocal language behavior.

The game of BLITZ is best played by four individuals or four teams. Each individual/team chooses a game piece (representing one of the four colors) and places it on the matching color-coded START field corner marked with an X. After rolling a six, the individual/team can begin play. The number shown on the second roll of the die indicates how many fields an individual/team can move forward. If, for example, the field is red, the top card from the stack of red cards is drawn and read to all the other players/teams. If green, the top card from the green stack is read and so on. The individual/team will then have to answer the card with the appropriate response. Should the response be inaccu-rate, the individual/team is penalized by returning to the playing field prior to the roll of the die. Conversely, an individual/team can remain on the new field if the response is correct, and the next individual/team takes a turn.

In addition, if an individual/team throws a six or lands on a designated BLITZ field, then the individual/team progresses to the new field with-out having to answer a card while receiving a bonus round for a second throw. On the new field of the second throw, however, the individual/team has to answer the card. If the answer is deemed correct, the indi-vidual/team remains on that field; if incorrect, the individual/team must return to the BLITZ field or to the field prior to the second roll of the die. The game comes to an end after an individual/team reaches the designated triangular END zone in the center of Path 3.

Regardless of outcome, all players/teams involved in this game board come away with a sense of accomplishment and satisfaction for knowledge, new or reviewed. During play time, the resourceful instructor monitors students' performance and mediates disagreements upon request.

Conclusion

Although games will continue to be used by language professionals to meet different needs for different groups of learners, those that adhere to well-established principles of learning will without a doubt have the most profound impact on second language learners. Ultimately, such learning games will enable resourceful language teachers to approach the teaching and learning of the target language and culture playfully but with a learning purpose in mind, for playing with a purpose is but one gateway to achieving proficiency in the second language classroom today and in the years ahead.

Notes

[1]   I wish to thank Professor Ursula Williams for reading and commenting on an earlier version of this article. Any remaining errors are, of course, the responsibility of the author.

References

Ahmad, J. (1981). The game's the thing. *Hispania, 64* (3), 401-403.

Alsop, T. W. (1980). Grand Prix wagon racing: Speaking the language–Having fun. *Foreign Language Annals, 13* (1), 57-58.

American Council on the Teaching of Foreign Languages. (1986). *ACTFL proficiency guidelines*. Hastings-on-Hudson, NY: American Council on the Teaching of Foreign Languages.

Arnold, R. A. (1979). The function of language games in the classroom. *English Language Teaching Journal, 33* (3), 205-207.

Berman, M. (1980). Word games. *English Language Teaching Journal, 34* (3), 213-215.

Buehler, G. (1979). The *Pyramidenspiel* as class or club learning endeavor. *Die Unterrichtspraxis, 2*, 73-77.

Crookall, D., & Oxford, R. (1989). (Eds.). *Language learning through simulation/gaming*. New York: Newbury House/Harper & Row.

Culley, G. (1986). A foreign language adventure game: Progress report on an application of AI to language instruction. *CALICO Journal, 4* (2), 69-87.

Danesi, M. (1987). *Puzzles and games in language teaching*. Lincolnwood, IL: National Textbook Company.

Hacken, R. D. (1979). Blackboard baseball. *Die Unterrichtspraxis, 1*, 69-71.

Hubp, L. B. (1974). *Let's play games in Spanish*. Skokie, IL: National Textbook Company.

Kaiser, L. (1977). Easy games for the German classroom. *Die Unterrichtspraxis, 10* (2), 122-127.

Lafayette, R.C. (Ed.) (1996). *National standards:A catalyst for reform.* Lincolnwood, IL: National Textbook Company.

Lange, D. L. (1999). Planning for using the new national culture standards. In J. Phillips & R. M. Terry (Eds.), *Foreign language standards: Linking research, theories, and practices* (pp. 57-120). Lincolnwood, IL: National Textbook Company.

Lee, W. R. (1979). *Language teaching games and contests*. 2nd ed. New York, NY: Oxford University Press.

Liontas, J. I. (1992). TELE-QUICK and the TELEPEDIA approach to teaching and learning German: A Lernvergnügen experience. *Schatzkammer, 18* (1), 63-85.

Liontas, J. I. (1992). Developing proficiency-based game approaches. In R. M. Terry (Ed.), *Dimension '91: Making a world of difference* (pp. 115-125). Valdosta, GA: Southern Conference on Language Teaching.

Lynch, M. (1986). Trivial pursuit in the foreign language classroom. In *Dimension '84-'85: Perspectives on proficiency: Curriculum and instruction* (pp. 153-157). Columbia, SC: Southern Conference on Language Teaching.

Matheidez, M. (1988). Games for language learning. In D. Saunders, A. Coote, & D. Crookall (Eds.), *Learning from experience through games and simulations* (pp. 72-75). Loughborough: SAGSET.

National Standards in Foreign Language Education Project. (1996). *Standards for foreign language learning: Preparing for the 21ˢᵗ century.* Lawrence, KS: Allen Press.

Omaggio, A. C. (1978). *Games and simulations in the foreign language classroom*. Arlington, VA: Center for Applied Linguistics.

Omaggio, A. C. (1982). Using games and simulations for the development of functional proficiency in a second language. *Canadian Modern Language Review, 38* (3), 517-546.

Schmidt, E. (1977). *Let's play games in German.* Lincolnwood, IL: National Textbook Company.

Siskin, H. J., & Spinelli, E. (1987). Achieving communicative competence through gambits and routines. *Foreign Language Annals, 20*, 393-401.

Smith, C. R. (1981). Contextualizing pattern drills: The 'German circle games.' *Foreign Language Annals, 14* (3), 203-212.

Wright, A, Betteridge, D., & Buckby, M. (1984). *Games for language learning.* Cambridge: Cambridge University Press.

Wright, M. (1989). Language Crafter: A foreign language word processor and word game package. *Hispania, 72* (3), 792-795.

Figure 1: *ZOOMANIA Game Card*

Figure 2: *BLITZ Game Card*

10
Oh, What a Tangled Web …
Teaching Foreign Languages Online

Karen Hardy Cárdenas
South Dakota State University

The newspaper headline read, "[Governor] Janklow Pitches Web-based Education." To anyone who knows the Governor of South Dakota, the headline should have come as no surprise. However, the dateline of Washington, D. C. was surprising. Governor Janklow's efforts to network the state have rarely attracted nationwide attention. The article reported that South Dakota Governor Bill Janklow had told a congressional subcommittee that, "Technology is able to level the divide." He also said, "My vision is a computer terminal on every desk, with high-speed Internet access." The subcommittee, chaired by Senator Bob Kerrey of Nebraska, was charged with making recommendations to the President on "how to ensure equal and affordable access to Web-based educational opportunities" (Frommer, 2000).

The article did not specifically mention foreign languages. But most foreign language educators would acknowledge that distance learning, using a variety of technologies, impacts them specifically. Foreign language classes, both at the secondary and the college/university level, tend to be small. Enrollments are often too small for a single school to offer advanced classes, and using technology to combine small classes is attractive to many administrators (Cárdenas, 1998a). Nor should technology hold any surprises or threats for foreign language educators. Since the days of the reel-to-reel tape recorder and language laboratory assignments, teachers of foreign languages have been using overhead transparencies, slides, videos, audio tapes, compact disks, web-sites, and PowerPoint presentations to enhance students' learning experiences of language and culture. But there is something different about teaching a foreign language on the Web.

Certainly one of the most important differences might be labeled "The Politics of the Web." If teachers decide to play a tape of Carlos Gardel in order to enhance students' appreciation of the tango or bring in slides of Madrid to show students the Plaza Mayor, they are making choices about how they believe students learn best. But if teachers are directed to develop web courses in elementary French or German on the premise that the Web is the teaching medium of the future, they are not being given choices. In fact, they are being ordered to do something which may be totally alien to what they believe is right (Cárdenas, 1998a; Cárdenas, 1998b).

Why are teachers being urged, if not forced, to use the Web as the primary (if not the only) means of delivering foreign language instruction? This is perhaps a political question. Administrators have bought into the Web (and, to some extent, other technologies) as the panacea to all problems. Phrases like "leveling the playing field," "equal access," and "an education free of time and place" are used to support administrators' insistence that classes, even foreign language classes, should be available online.

This phenomenon is a relatively recent one, but not so recent that it has not already inspired a backlash. In an article posted on the Web, James R. Mingle, Executive Director of the State Higher Education Executive Officers, notes the number of states that have allocated vast amounts of money to technology. In his 1997 article, he cautions that investments in technology can be justified only if they result in improved student learning. He goes on to say, "Without learning gains ... technology may prove to be part of the cost problem and not the productivity solution" (Mingle, 1997).

Two other authors have voiced concerns about the tendency to consider technology as the cure to all of education's problems. Ed Neal, in a 1998 issue of *The Chronicle of Higher Education*, notes that teachers have been through the Web hype before. In the '60s they were told to develop courses for television since it was believed that, in the future, at least half of all classes would be on television. He also mentions the fact that high-level administrators are frequently looking for a way to leave their mark on a campus (before heading off to their next position), and technology has become one popular way to do so (Neal, 1998).

Jane M. Healy, in her book *Failure to Connect*, notes that we have a need to believe that computers will solve all of our problems. She quotes William Ruckeyser on the widespread belief in the efficacy of computers, "The nearest thing I can draw a parallel to is a theological discussion. There's so much an element of faith here that demanding evidence is almost a sign of heresy" (Healy, 1998).

If administrators at the secondary and the college/university level are demanding that teachers, including foreign language teachers, develop web courses, one reason may be the popularity of something called the "No Significant Difference" theory. This theory, as its name suggests, argues that there is no significant difference between classroom learning and online learning. There is even a web site devoted to this theory ("No Significant Difference"). (The author has, in fact, heard a number of administrators tout the excellence of web courses by insisting that students, in any and all disciplines, learn better on the web than in a traditional setting.)

When one reads the results of studies cited on the "No Significant Difference" web site, it is hard to contradict the evidence provided. One teacher after another cites the results of studies that compare classroom students with others who took the same course online, indicating that there is little if any difference between the performance of the two groups. In some cases, the online students may have even done better than the in-class students.

However, foreign language teachers will find few studies relating to their discipline on this web site. A close scrutiny of the research reported on the "No Significant Difference" web site tends to show that the studies reported are limited to very specific disciplines and to very definite groups of learners. The disciplines are, most frequently, the hard sciences, and the learners tend to be older, established learners or non-traditional learners. Foreign language teachers seeking confirmation that web-based learning is a viable option for their students will be disappointed.

It is to the credit of the proponents of the "No Significant Difference" theory that their web site directs the researcher to another site called the "Significant Difference" site. This latter site is devoted to contradicting the assertion that there is no difference between classroom learning and online learning. On this particular site, one can read a very substantial report prepared by The Institute for Higher Education Policy on behalf of the American Federation of Teachers and the National Education Association ("What's the Difference?" 1998).

This 30-page, very well documented report entitled "What's the Difference?" does not attempt to dispute the claims of the proponents of the "No Significant Difference" theory. However, it reviews the research to date and points to key shortcomings and gaps in the research. In the section entitled "Implications," the authors cite "three broad implications that can be derived from [their] review of the ... research."

The first of the implications is that "the notion of 'access to [education]' in the distance learning context is unclear." The second is "that technology cannot replace the human factor in ... education." And third, "many of the results [of the research] seem to indicate that technology is not nearly as important as other factors" ("What's the Difference?" pp. 7-8).

Regarding the first implication, access to education, the authors of the study note that, "Many of the advocates of distance learning tout access to ... education as a *raison d'être* for the proliferation of distance education. Indeed, in some states, public policy leaders are recommending using distance education in lieu of 'bricks and mortar' learning" (What's the Difference?" p. 7). The authors note that there are various questions that need to be answered before web-based courses are peddled as the solution to access to higher education.

One concern is with quality: Does a web-based course give students an educational experience that has the same quality as a traditional classroom-based course? Other concerns relate to the mechanics of web-based distance learning. To take advantage of web-based courses, students must have computers and know how to use them. They must also have access to technical support when it is needed. Today, the fact is that all students do not have equal access to higher education through Web courses because they lack the equipment and the knowledge necessary.

Another concern, and perhaps the most important, is that no technology can replace a teacher. It is not enough that a web course be designed and developed by a competent professional. That professional, the teacher, must remain involved in on-going interaction with students to insure that the goals of the course are being met. This concern is very legitimate, since the literature documents a number of instances in which unemployed faculty members are being hired to write courses that are subsequently graded by teaching assistants.

A final concern is with how technology affects student learning and student satisfaction. The findings here are very important. The results "seem to indicate that technology is not nearly as important as other factors, such as learning tasks, learner characteristics, student motivation and the instructor." The research in this area seems to support an allegation made in the title of an article in *DEOSNEWS*: "Good Teaching Is Good Teaching" (Ragan, 1998).

So, what is a foreign language teacher to do in the face of demand for online courses and evidence that there are limitations and potential problems with such courses? Tempting though it may be, deciding to have nothing to do with such courses is not a realistic option. If competent professionals refuse to develop good courses based on sound pedagogy, there is a possibility that administrators will seek out foreign language courses elsewhere.

Even if that possibility is not a threat, foreign language teachers should explore distance-learning options, including web courses. Why? In a 1997 speech to the Washington Higher Education Secretariat, Sir John Daniel, Vice Chancellor of England's Open University, posed the question: "If technology is the answer, what is the question?"(Daniel, 1997). His opening provoked laughter from the group, but his answer was very sobering. He provided a detailed account of the many parts of the world where people have virtually no access to the education that would bring them better jobs and bring their countries increased prosperity.

In many developing regions, there simply aren't enough centers of higher learning to train the engineers and scientists needed for the countries to progress economically. This plight is the reason that the Open University provides instruction in an amazing number of fields through correspondence and web courses. Even though these particular countries might not need language classes, the fact remains that technology is a way to reach students who do need foreign language classes, but cannot come to a university campus.

Currently in South Dakota, the individuals in greatest need of web courses are students are at the upper-division level and in-service teachers in need of professional development. Without distance education in general, and web courses in particular, many students in sparsely populated states may be denied the opportunity to take a wide range of upper-division courses. Further, in-service teachers may be obligated to take courses unrelated to their major teaching field in order to recertify.

Web courses are still not common in most foreign languages, and there are few models to follow. However, several organizations that focus on distance learning have developed general guidelines to help the individual who is creating a web course. The American Center for the Study of Distance Education, the American Distance Education Consortium, and the Western Interstate Commission for Higher Education, among others, provide guidelines to people interested in putting a course on the web (ACSDE, ADEC, WICHE Guidelines).

By drawing from all of these sources, the following Ten Commandments of web teaching are proposed:

1. Web courses will be designed and taught by a professional in the field. Ideally the same teacher will teach the course who designed the course. When that arrangement is not possible, the designer will be responsible for providing direction for those teaching the course to insure that the goals of the course are being met.

2. The same rules that restrict traditional classroom sizes shall also hold true for a web course. Just because there is no physical limitation of space, an upper-division web course cannot accommodate 100 students.
3. Learning goals will be clearly articulated, and all activities will be designed to help students achieve these goals.
4. A web course will entail as wide a variety of interactions as possible.
5. Students will be prepared to use all the technologies required in the web course.
6. Assignments given will be appropriate to the subject matter being taught and will also be appropriate to the medium of instruction.
7. Assessment will be ongoing, consistent with learning goals, and appropriate to the teaching medium.
8. Technologies used will be appropriate for the course and will be consistent with the learning objectives of the web course.
9. Faculty who design and deliver web courses shall have proper institutional support.
10. Students who take web courses shall have continuous, uninterrupted access to technical support.

Volumes could be (and probably will be) written about any one of these "commandments." But, commandment number 4 is absolutely key to the success of a web course; thus, it will be explored in greater depth.

At an ACTFL conference several years ago, there was a session on designing web courses, and many people attended hoping to get some guidance in this uncharted terrain. It was somewhat surprising that one of the speakers gave the following outline of his course: "Well, first they read the literary selection online. Then I have a series of vocabulary exercises on the difficult words in the selection. Then they have short-answer questions and longer discussion questions, and finally they write an essay on what they've read."

As an attendee at this session, I found myself totally disappointed by this outline of activities. I designed and taught correspondence courses in the mid-eighties and even under the constraints of the correspondence course medium, I managed to do better than that. In a 1997 publication of *Distance Education: An International Journal*, there is an article that speaks to this issue. It is entitled "Best and Worst Dressed Web Courses: Strutting into the 21st Century in Comfort and Style" (Boshier, Mohapi, Moulton, Qayyum, Sadownik, & Wilson, 1997).

According to the authors, "… some courses are vastly under-dressed and merely attempt to display a face-to-face course online. At the other extreme are those laced with links, animation and more than enough glitter and glam to make Liberace wince" (Boshier, et al, 1997). Not only was the course I heard described at ACTFL "underdressed," it would have been unacceptable if it had been a traditional classroom-based course.

An "overdressed" course, on the other hand, might flaunt cute cartoons (some of them in vivid color and with animation) and emoticons on every page. Although such courses display the creator's ingenuity, they do little to enhance the learning process. Furthermore, the use of cartoons and emoticons eventually becomes distracting.

So, what kinds of interactions could be used in a foreign language web course? Let us start by saying that web courses in foreign languages are best when they involve students who already have a fundamental knowledge of the language. Such courses should be knowledge-based and designed to refine skills, rather than geared toward teaching a student the fundamentals of the language. In the future, there is no doubt that technology will be sophisticated enough to permit the effective teaching of German 101 online. But that day has not yet come.

Let us suppose that students are studying contemporary Latin American culture. They will be required to buy a textbook and will have to purchase or download a study guide. At regular intervals, they will need to send their instructor answers to specific questions that demonstrate that they understand the basics of what they have read.

Already we have two kinds of interaction taking place, pedestrian though they may be. We have interaction between the student and a body of material as well as interaction between the student and instructor. But, if this is all the course entails, it might as well be a correspondence course.

What else could these students in a web course do to develop their knowledge of the subject matter and also to hone their communication skills? Suppose the students have read about the ethnic composition of various Latin American countries and the problems of economic development in Latin America, but they have not really made these issues their own. So, they might be asked to respond in Spanish to a number of discussion questions on these issues as well as be asked to respond to their classmates' comments on these same issues.

The course textbook used may speak of generalities regarding the Hispanic world. But what is going on today in Latin America? tudents might be asked to engage in online research on current Latin American events.

They could direct their classmates (webmates) to go to a particular site and to offer comments on the information it contains. Other students could subsequently comment on their classmates' (webmates') observations.

In lieu of formal exams, students might develop portfolios that contain all the documents they have prepared for the course. These portfolios could include answers to content questions, comments on discussion questions, web sites where articles of interest regarding Latin America are found, and other documents. For example, in a recent online course, one student provided web addresses of sites related to the major topics being studied in the class. Some of these sites were very useful to other students in the class.

Many of the programs that are used to develop web courses (WebCT, Web Course in a Box, Lotus Notes) also recommend that there be a place in the web course (the cafeteria, the student union) where students can talk to each other about subjects that do not directly pertain to the course. Many programs also encourage students to develop personal web pages so they can let their webmates know who they are. The author has not found that asking students to communicate with one another has fostered the kind of community that one hopes to build during a web course. But to the extent that creating personal connections between and among students can improve their online interactions, this community should be encouraged.

Web courses are still a relatively new phenomenon, particularly in the field of foreign languages. In some instances, faculty members are being urged by administrators to develop such courses at various levels. Developing a web course that provides students with an experience comparable to the one they would receive in a traditional classroom environment is not easy. But, if we are to reach the students who need this information and who cannot travel to campus, the effort is worthwhile.

References

American Distance Education Consortium. (1998). *ADEC guiding principles for distance teaching and learning* [Online]. Available: http://www.adec.edu/admin/papers/distance-teaching_principles.html

The American Center for the Study of Distance Education. (2000). *Internet-based distance education bibliography 1997-1999* [Online]. Available: http://www/ed.psu.edu/acsde/annbib/parta.asp

Boshier, R., Mohapi, M., Moulton, G., Qayyam, A., Sadownik, L., & Wilson, M. (1997). Best and worst dressed web courses: Strutting into the 21st century in comfort and style. *Distance Education–An International Journal, 18* (2), 327-348.

Cárdenas, K. H. (1998a). Saving small foreign language programs: Is cooperation the answer? *AFDL Bulletin, 29* (3), 11-19.

Cárdenas, K. H. (1998b). Technology in today's classroom: It slices and it dices, but does it serve us well? *Academe, 8* (May-June), 27-29.

Cárdenas, K. H. (2000). Technology in higher education: Issues for the new millennium. In J. Losco & B. L. Fife, *Higher education in transition: The challenges of the new millennium.* Westport, CT: Bergin and Garvey.

College Board. (1999). The virtual university and educational opportunity: Issues of equity and access for the next generation [Online]. Available: http://www.collegeboard.org/policy/html/virtual.html

Council for Higher Education Accreditation. (2000). Distance learning in higher education. *CHEA Update,* No. 3 [Online]. Available: http://www.chea.org/Commentary/distance-learning-3.cfm

Frommer, F. J. (2000). "Janklow pitches web-based education: Daschle touts governor's vision before Panel." *Argus Leader*, Sioux Falls, South Dakota, September 15, 5B.

Healy, J. M. (1998). *Failure to connect: How computers affect our children's minds–for better and worse.* New York: Simon and Schuster.

The Institute for Higher Education Policy. (1999). *What's the difference? A review of contemporary research on the effectiveness of distance learning in higher education* [Online]. Available: http://www.ihep.com

Mingle J. R. (1997). *New technology funds: Problem or solution?* [Online]. Available: http://www.sheeo.org

Moore, M. G., & Cozine, G. T. (Eds.). (2000). Web-based communications, the internet and distance education. *Readings in Distance Education Series,* No. 7 [Online]. Available: http://www.ed.psu.edu/acsde/readings/read.asp#No.%206

Neal, E. (1998). Using technology in teaching: We need to exercise healthy skepticism. *The Chronicle of Higher Education,* June 19, B4-B5.

No significant difference phenomenon [Online]. Available: http://cuda.teleeducation.nb.ca/nosignificantdifference/

Project ADEPT. (2000). *Assessment of distance education pedagogy and technology website* [Online]. Available: http://www.users.csbsju.edu/~tcreed/adept/

Ragan, L.C. (1998). Good teaching is good teaching: An emerging set of guiding principles and practices for the design and development of distance education. *DEOS (Distance Education Online) NEWS, 8* (12).

Significant difference [Online]. Available: http://cuda.teleeducation.nb.ca/significantdifference

Western Interstate Commission for Higher Education. (1999). Principles of good practice for electronically offered academic degree and certificate programs [Online]. Available: http://www.wiche.edu/Telecom/projects/balancing/principles.htm